THiNK

A2

WORKBOOK 1

Herbert Puchta, Jeff Stranks & Peter Lewis-Jones

T0349705

CAMBRIDGE
UNIVERSITY PRESS

Acknowledgements

The authors and publishers acknowledge the following sources of copyright material and are grateful for the permissions granted. While every effort has been made, it has not always been possible to identify the sources of all the material used, or to trace all copyright holders. If any omissions are brought to our notice, we will be happy to include the appropriate acknowledgements on reprinting.

Emily Cummins for the text on p. 68 adapted from http://www.emilycummins. co.uk/about. Copyright © Emily Cummins. Reproduced with permission.

Corpus
Development of this publication has made use of the Cambridge English Corpus (CEC). The CEC is a computer database of contemporary spoken and written English, which currently stands at over one billion words. It includes British English, American English and other varieties of English. It also includes the Cambridge Learner Corpus, developed in collaboration with Cambridge English Language Assessment. Cambridge University Press has built up the CEC to provide evidence about language use that helps to produce better language teaching materials.

English Profile
This product is informed by the English Vocabulary Profile, built as part of English Profile, a collaborative programme designed to enhance the learning, teaching and assessment of English worldwide. Its main funding partners are Cambridge University Press and Cambridge English Language Assessment and its aim is to create a 'profile' for English linked to the Common European Framework of Reference for Languages (CEF). English Profile outcomes, such as the English Vocabulary Profile, will provide detailed information about the language that learners can be expected to demonstrate at each CEF level, offering a clear benchmark for learners' proficiency. For more information, please visit
www.englishprofile.org

Cambridge Dictionaries
Cambridge dictionaries are the world's most widely used dictionaries for learners of English. The dictionaries are available in print and online at dictionary.cambridge.org. Copyright © Cambridge University Press, reproduced with permission.

The publishers are grateful to the following for permission to reproduce copyright photographs and material:

T = Top, B = Below, L = Left, R = Right, C = Centre, B/G = Background

p. 8 (T): ©patpitchaya/iStock/360/Getty Images; p. 8 (1): ©Oleksiy Mark/ iStock/360/Getty Images; p. 8 (2): ©Ameng Wu/iStock /360/Getty Images; p. 8 (3): ©Duygun VURAL/iStock/360/Getty Images; p. 8 (4): ©hamurishi/ iStock/360/Getty Images; p. 8 (5): ©studionobra/iStock/360/Getty Images; p. 8 (6): ©AleksVF/iStock/360/Getty Images; p. 14 (TL): ©Joe McBride/Iconica/ Getty Images; p. 14 (TR): ©DAJ/Getty Images; p. 14 (BL): ©Yvette Cardozo/ Alamy; p. 15 (T): ©bevangoldswain/iStock/360/Getty Images; p. 15 (BL): ©Jose Luis Pelaez Inc/Getty Images; p. 15 (BR): ©Kovalchuk Oleksandr/Shutterstock; p. 20 (L): ©Avatar_023/Shutterstock; p. 20 (CL): ©PhotoAlto/Laurence Mouton/ Brand X Pictures/Getty Images; p. 20 (C): ©StockLite/Shutterstock; p. 20 (CR): ©Patrick Breig/Shutterstock; p. 20 (R): ©Denkou Images/Cultura/Getty Images; p. 21 (TL): ©Didecs/Shutterstock; p. 21 (TR): ©IvonneW/iStock/360/Getty Images; p. 21 (CL): ©vuvu/Shutterstock; p. 21 (CR): ©Zoonar RF/Zoonar/360/ Getty Images; p. 21 (BL): ©Tatiana Popova/Shutterstock; p. 21 (BR): ©Oleksiy Mark/iStock/360/Getty Images; p. 22 (T): ©Radius/Superstock; p. 22 (B): ©Hero Images/Getty Images; p. 24: ©Fuse/Getty Images; p. 26 (TL, BR): ©Eduardo Jose Bernardino/iStock/360/Getty Images; p. 26 (TR): ©jodiejohnson/iStock/360/ Getty Images; p. 26 (BL): ©C. Diane O'Keefe/iStock/360/Getty Images; p. 27: ©saras66/Shutterstock; p. 31 (TL): ©Sergio Martinez/Shutterstock; p. 31 (TC): ©ULKASTUDIO/Shutterstock; p. 31 (TR): ©Nattika/Shutterstock; p. 31 (CL): ©rimglow/iStock/360/Getty Images; p. 31 (C): ©Bozena Fulawka/Shutterstock; p. 31 (CR): ©Meelena/Shutterstock; p. 31 (BL): ©Viktor1/Shutterstock; p. 31 (BC): ©gmevi/iStock/360/Getty Images; p. 31 (BR): ©voltan1/iStock/360/Getty Images; p. 32 (TL): ©chengyuzheng/iStock/360/Getty Images; p. 32 (TR): ©anankkml/ iStock/360/Getty Images; p. 32 (CL): ©Steve Lenz/iStock/360/Getty Images; p. 32 (CR): ©Eric Isselée/iStock/360/Getty Images; p. 32 (BL): ©xstockerx/Shutterstock;

p. 32 (BR): ©StockSolutions/iStock/360/Getty Images; p. 33: ©killerbayer/ iStock/360/Getty Images; p. 34: ©Adam Hester/Corbis; p. 40: ©Pankaj & Insy Shah/Getty Images; p. 42 (TL, BL): ©Vtls/Shutterstock; p. 42 (TR, BR): ©White Smoke/Shutterstock; p. 50 (T): ©epa/Corbis; p. 50 (C): ©Ralf-Finn Hestoft/ CORBIS; p. 50 (B): ©AFP/Getty Images; p. 51 (L): ©DenisKotr/iStock/360/Getty Images; p. 51 (CL): ©sagir/Shutterstock; p. 51 (C): ©Ad Oculos/Shutterstock; p. 51 (CR): ©Room27/Shutterstock; p. 51 (R): ©bopav/Shutterstock; p. 55: ©AFP/ Getty Images; p. 58 (TR): ©UNITED ARTISTS/THE KOBAL COLLECTION; p. 58 (TL): ©Pictorial Press Ltd/Alamy; p. 58 (B): ©REX/Everett Collection; p. 60: ©REX/ Geoffrey Swaine; p. 63: ©diego cervo/iStock/360/Getty Images; p. 68 (TL): ©REX/Ray Tang; p. 68 (TR): ©Emily Cummins http://www.emilycummins.co.uk; p. 68 (B): ©Emily Cummins http://www.emilycummins.co.uk; p. 69 (TL): ©BrAt82/ Shutterstock; p. 69 (TR): ©BuddyFly/iStock/360/Getty Images; p. 69 (CL): ©REX/Roger Viollet; p. 69 (CR): ©George Timakov/Hemera/360/Getty Images; p. 69 (B): ©akajhoe/iStock/360/Getty Images; p. 75 (snowboard): ©YanLev/ Shutterstock; p. 75 (golf): ©anek_s/iStock/360/Getty Images; p. 75 (windsurf): ©jan kranendonk/iStock/360/Getty Images; p. 75 (volleyball): ©Eastimages/ Shutterstock; p. 75 (skis and poles): ©gorillaimages/Shutterstock; p. 75 (football): ©stockphoto-graf/Shutterstock; p. 75 (diving board): ©sirastock/Shutterstock; p. 75 (helmet and rope): ©grafvision/Shutterstock; p. 75 (parallel bars): ©versh/ Shutterstock; p. 75 (sailing): ©Michael Blann/Photodisc/Getty Images; p. 75 (starting block): ©Ulrich Mueller/Shutterstock; p. 75 (rugby): ©Paolo De santis/ Hemera/360/Getty Images; p. 75 (tennis): ©miflippo/iStock/360/Getty Images; p. 76 (TR): ©technotr/E+/Getty Images; p. 76 (TL): ©Keystone/Hulton Archive/ Getty Images; p. 76 (BR): ©YTopFoto; p. 76 (BL): ©Tony Duffy/Getty Images Sport/Getty Images; p. 77: ©Galina Burtseva/iStock/360/Getty Images; p. 78 (TL): ©Echo/Cultura/Getty Images; p. 78 (TC): ©The Washington Post/Getty Images; p. 78 (TR): ©Konstantin Shishkin/iStock/360/Getty Images; p. 78 (CL): ©LuckyBusiness/iStock/360/Getty Images; p. 78 (C): ©Kzenon/Shutterstock; p. 78 (CR): ©Greg Epperson/iStock/360/Getty Images; p. 78 (BL): ©Ingram Publishing/Getty Images; p. 78 (BC): ©saintho/iStock/360/Getty Images; p. 78 (BR): ©Jupiterimages/Stockbyte/Getty Images; p. 79: ©Athol Pictures/ Alamy; p. 81: ©JUNG YEON-JE /AFP/Getty Images; p. 86: ©Yvette Cardozo/ Photolibrary/Getty Images; p. 87: ©Barry Mason/Alamy; p. 92 (zebra crossing): ©Stephen Rees/Shutterstock; p. 92 (youth club): ©Jeff Morgan 16/Alamy; p. 92 (speed camera): ©Howard_M/iStock/360/Getty Images; p. 92 (graffiti): ©A_Lesik/Shutterstock; p. 92 (cycle lane): ©Aleramo/iStock/360/Getty Images; p. 92 (litter bin): ©sunsetman/Shutterstock; p. 92 (bill board): ©Jeff Morgan 09/Alamy; p. 92 (high street): ©Ingram Publishing/Getty Images; p. 92 (skate park): ©moodboard/360/getty Images; p. 94 (TL): ©RICK WILKING/Reuters/ Corbis; p. 94 (TR): ©Claver Carroll/Photolibrary/Getty Images; p. 94 (C): ©ArtPix/Alamy; p. 94 (B): ©Gideon Mendel/Corbis; p. 95: ©David Hughes/ Hemera/360/Getty Images; p. 99: ©OlgaCanals/iStock/360/Getty Images; p. 102 (BL): ©vadimmmus/iStock/360/Getty Images; p. 102 (TL): ©Holger Scheibe/ Corbis; p. 102 (stomachache): ©Shutterstock/Photographee.eu; p. 102 (earache): ©Shutterstock/Dora Zett; p. 102 (headache): ©ATIC12/iStock/360/Getty Images; p. 102 (toothache): ©Thomas Lammeyer/Herma/360/Getty Images; p. 104 (L): ©Eric Fleming Photography/Shutterstock; p. 104 (R): ©Rich Carey/Shutterstock; p. 111 (1): ©JackF/iStock/360/Getty Images; p. 111 (2): ©Onoky/Supersock; p. 111 (3): ©Kimberly Brotherman/Moment Open/Getty Images; p. 111 (4): ©KatPaws/iStock/360/Getty Images; p. 111 (5): ©Matthew Grant/iStock/360/ Getty Images; p. 111 (6): ©Marin Tomas/iStock/360/Getty Images; p. 111 (7): ©Charles O. Cecil/Alamy; p. 111 (8): ©Shutterstock/Dudarev Mikhail; p. 111 (9): ©hxdyl/iStock/360/Getty Images.

Cover photographs by: (L): ©Yuliya Koldovska/Shutterstock; (TR): ©Tim Gainey/ Alamy; (BR): ©Oliver Burston/Alamy.

The publishers are grateful to the following illustrators:
David Semple 5, 18, 20, 29, 37, 38, 39, 52, 67, 73, 88, 101, 108; Fred Van Deelen (The Organisation) 7, 25, 62, 64, 93; Julian Mosedale 16, 19, 21, 31, 38, 42, 59, 70, 82, 91, 103, 112

The publishers are grateful to the following contributors:
Blooberry Design Ltd: text design and layouts; Claire Parson: cover design; Hilary Fletcher: picture research; Leon Chambers: audio recordings; Karen Elliott: Pronunciation sections; Diane Nicholls: Get it right! exercises

CONTENTS

WELCOME

A ALL ABOUT ME
Personal information

1 Match the sentences and the replies.

1	What's your name? ☐	a	I'm 14.
2	How old are you? ☐	b	Hi, Lucy, I'm Laura.
3	Where are you from? ☐	c	Hi, Jim. Nice to meet you.
4	Hi, I'm Lucy. ☐	d	Nice to meet you, too.
5	This is my friend Jim. ☐	e	My name's Steve.
6	Nice to meet you. ☐	f	I'm from Hereford in England.

2 Write <u>your</u> answers to questions 1–3 in Exercise 1.

1 _____
2 _____
3 _____

Nationalities and *be*

1 Find 12 countries in the word search.

```
T C O L O M B I A O N
K J C M Z F I U A R E
A R G E N T I N A Y T
T K T X T Y U O U E H
L N U I K L U Y W A E
P I R C O L U M B I R
N A K O A Y I E J S L
C T E U P L P W N S A
X I Y S P A I N F U N
A R N A U T T M P R D
O B R A Z I L D M O S
P A L R M U I G L E B
```

2 Complete with the verb *to be*.

0 It *'s* a Ferrari.
1 They _____ from Moscow.
2 I _____ (not) from London.
3 _____ Paula from New York?
4 _____ you from São Paulo?
5 We _____ (not) from Barcelona.
6 Augusto _____ from a small town near Buenos Aires.
7 My dad _____ (not) from Rome.

3 Match the sentences 0–7 in Exercise 2 with a–h.

a We're from Madrid. ☐
b They're Russian. ☐
c He's Argentinian. ☐
d But he is Italian. ☐
e Yes, I'm Brazilian. ☐
f It's an Italian car. ☐
g I'm from Liverpool. ☐
h Yes, she's American. ☐

4 Write the nationality of someone from ...

1 The Netherlands _____
2 Colombia _____
3 Mexico _____
4 Belgium _____
5 Turkey _____
6 Brazil _____
7 Argentina _____
8 Russia _____
9 Italy _____
10 The USA _____
11 Britain _____
12 Spain _____

Names and addresses

1 ◀))02 **Listen to the telephone conversation. Who is the man calling?**

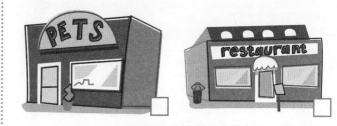

2 🔊02 **Listen again and complete the form.**

> # The Golden Duck
>
> Table for: ¹ _____
>
> Time: ² _____
>
> Name: ³ _____
>
> Contact number: ⁴ _____
>
> ⁵ _____ City Walls Road

3 🔊02 **Put the dialogue in order. Listen again and check.**

	MANAGER	OK, Mr Hodgson. And can I have a contact number?
	MANAGER	Sure, it's 22 City Walls Road.
	MANAGER	Could you spell that?
1	MANAGER	The Golden Duck. How can I help you?
	MANAGER	A table for four at 8 pm. Can I have your name?
	MANAGER	Thank you. See you later tonight, Mr Hodgson.
	MR HODGSON	Just one more thing. Can you give me your address?
	MR HODGSON	It's Hodgson. Bob Hodgson.
	MR HODGSON	Sure. It's H - O - D - G - S - O - N.
	MR HODGSON	Hello, I'd like to book a table for four for tonight about 8 pm.
	MR HODGSON	Yes, it's 0796 38888.

SUMMING UP

1 Complete the text with the verb *to be* and the nationalities.

My favourite football team has players in it from all over the world.
Costa and Nunes ¹_____ from Rio de Janeiro.
They ²_____ ³_____ .
Ramos ⁴_____ from Bogotá. He ⁵_____
⁶_____ .
Simenon ⁷_____ ⁸_____ . He ⁹_____
from Brussels.
Jones and Lalas ¹⁰_____ ¹¹_____ . Jones
¹²_____ from New York and Lalas ¹³_____
from Miami.
The other players ¹⁴_____ ¹⁵_____ . They
¹⁶_____ from lots of different cities in Britain.

B WHAT'S THAT?

Things in the classroom and prepositions of place

1 Find and (circle) 12 classroom items in the word snake.

doorboardrulerfloorcdnotebookwindowpenbookchairpencildesk

2 Complete with the classroom objects in the list.

ruler | teacher | chair | pen | board | notebook

1 The _____ is under the chair.
2 The _____ is behind the desk.
3 The _____ is on the desk.
4 The _____ is in front of the board.
5 The _____ is between the door and the window.
6 The _____ is on a book.

Classroom language

1 Put the words in order to make sentences.

1 I / a / can / question /ask / ?

_____

2 again / can / say / that / you / ?

_____

3 page / your / open / at / 10 / books

_____

4 don't / I / know

_____

5 I / understand / don't

_____

6 mean / word / does / what / this / ?

_____

7 that / do / word / spell / you / how / ?

_____

8 English / how / say / amanhã / in / do / you / ?

_____

9 if / hands / your / know / up / answer / put / you / the

_____

Object pronouns

1 Complete the table.

I	me
you	____
he	____
she	____
it	____
we	____
they	____

2 Circle the correct options in each sentence.

0 May's my best friend. I tell *she /* **her** everything.

1 *They / Them* don't speak English. That's why you don't understand *they / them.*

2 *I / Me* love this dress. Buy it for *I / me*, please.

3 Turn the music up. *We / Us* can't hear it.

4 Bob's got a problem and *I / me* can't help *he / him.*

5 *We / Us* love our gran. She gives *we / us* great presents on our birthdays.

3 Complete with the missing object pronoun.

0 I want my sandwich! Give it to ___me___.

1 That's Mr O'Brian. Say hello to _____.

2 Mum wants some help. Can you help _____?

3 I love _____. You're my best friend.

4 We really want to go to the show. Can you buy _____ some tickets?

5 The children are very noisy. Tell _____ to be quiet, please.

this, that, these, those

1 Circle the right words.

1 *This / These* homework is very difficult.

2 *That / Those* shoes are really nice.

3 *That / These* house is really old.

4 *These / This* books aren't very interesting.

2 Complete with *this, that, these* or *those*.

1 Can you pass me _____ books next to you, please?

2 Is _____ my pen in your hand?

3 _____ pencil is broken. Can you give me another one?

4 _____ shoes are too small for me. I need to take them off.

SUMMING UP

1 Complete the dialogue with the words in the list.

ask | know | spell | this | that
pen | say | notebook | put

ROBERTO   Excuse me, Miss Baker, can I [0] ___ask___ you a question?

MISS BAKER   Of course you can, Roberto.

ROBERTO   How do you [1]_____ 'pizza' in English?

MISS BAKER   Ahmed. Can you help?

AHMED   Sorry. I don't [2]_____ .

MISS BAKER   Can anyone help Roberto? [3]_____ your hands up if you know the answer. Yes, Kim.

KIM   It's easy. It's 'pizza'.

ROBERTO   How do you [4]_____ that?

KIM   P-I-Z-Z-A; it's the same as in Italian!

ROBERTO   OK, let me write that in my [5]_____ . Is [6]_____ your [7]_____? Can I borrow it?

KIM   No, [8]_____ 's your pen. You don't need to ask.

C ABOUT TIME
Days and dates

1 Sort the words into three different groups. There are four words in each group.

Sunday | October | fourteenth | third | July
Monday | second | tenth | March | Saturday
September | Friday

1 _____

2 _____

3 _____

2 Write the next word in each sequence.

1 February, April, June, _____

2 Friday, Thursday, Wednesday, _____

3 first, third, sixth, _____

4 1st, 10th, 19th, _____

5 April, August, December, _____

6 4th, 8th, 12th, _____

7 Monday, Wednesday, Friday, _____

8 December, November, October, _____

3 Write the numbers in words.

1 1st _____

2 4th _____

3 8th _____

4 11th _____

5 12th _____

6 15th _____

7 20th _____

8 22nd _____

9 25th _____

10 29th _____

11 30th _____

12 31st _____

4 Answer the questions.

When is …

1 your birthday?

_____

2 your country's national day?

_____

3 your best friend's birthday?

_____

4 the first day of your next school holiday?

_____

My day

1 Write the times on the clocks.

0 It's ____ *4 pm.* ____   1 It's _____

2 It's _____   3 It's _____

4 It's _____   5 It's _____

2 Read and put the events in order.

☐ I have lunch at quarter past one.

☐ I go to bed at twenty past eight.

☐ I go to school at seven o'clock.

☐ I have dinner at half past five.

☐ I have breakfast at quarter past six.

☐ I get home at half past one.

☐ *1* I get up at six o'clock.

☐ I do my homework at quarter to two.

3 Now write about your day.

1 *I get up at …* _____

2 _____

3 _____

4 _____

5 _____

6 _____

7 _____

8 _____

SUMMING UP

1 🔊03 **Listen and write the times that Dan does the following things.**

1 get up on Tuesday morning

_____

2 arrive at school

_____

3 get home after school

_____

4 go to bed

_____

5 get up on Sunday morning

_____

2 🔊03 **Put the dialogue in order. Listen and check.**

☐ ANA What!? Six o'clock!

☐ ANA Half past six in the morning? That's early. Why?

☐ ANA Oh. And what time does it finish?

☐ ANA So you love the weekend. You can get up late.

☐ ANA What do you do after lunch?

1 ANA What time do you get up, Dan?

☐ DAN Yes, six o'clock. I have early morning swimming lessons.

☐ DAN I do homework and watch TV. Sometimes I play football and basketball. Then it's dinner and I go to bed at nine o'clock.

☐ DAN Well, my school starts at seven o'clock.

☐ DAN Not at all. On Saturdays and Sundays I get up at six o'clock.

☐ DAN From Monday to Friday, I get up at half past six.

☐ DAN Twenty past twelve, so I get home at ten to one for lunch.

D MY THINGS
My possessions

1 Do the word puzzle and find the name of Jim's pet.

have got

1 Complete the sentences about Jim with *has* or *hasn't*. Use the previous exercise to help you.

1 Jim _____ got a lizard.

2 Jim _____ got a camera.

3 Jim _____ got a smartphone.

4 Jim _____ got a bike.

5 Jim _____ got a dog.

6 Jim _____ got a car.

2 Match the questions and the answers.

1 Have you got a pet? ☐
2 Has Jim got a cat? ☐
3 Have all your friends got smartphones? ☐
4 Has your brother got a bike? ☐
5 Have you got a lizard? ☐
6 Has Suzie got a brother? ☐

a Yes, they have.
b Yes, I've got a dog.
c No, he hasn't.
d No, she hasn't, but she's got a sister.
e No, I haven't.
f Yes, he has. It's called Mickey.

3 Circle the correct option.

1 I *have / has* got three brothers.
2 We *haven't / hasn't* got a car.
3 Susie *has / have* got a new phone.
4 They *haven't / hasn't* got any money.
5 James *haven't / hasn't* got homework tonight.
6 I *haven't / hasn't* got a pen. *Have / Has* you got one?

4 Complete the dialogue with *have, has, haven't* or *hasn't*.

BOB ¹_____ you got a laptop, Nick?

NICK No, I ²_____ but I'd love one.

BOB What about your brother? ³_____ he got one?

NICK Yes he ⁴_____ and he ⁵_____ got a tablet too.

BOB That's not fair.

NICK He's older than me. My sister ⁶_____ got one but she's only three.

BOB ⁷_____ your parents got a computer?

NICK Yes, they ⁸_____ . I use it sometimes.

5 Write sentences.

1 Two things you have got and two things you haven't got.

_____
_____
_____
_____

2 Two things your best friend has got and two things he/she hasn't got.

_____
_____
_____
_____

I like and *I'd like*

1 Circle the correct option.

1 A What's your favourite colour?
  B I *like / 'd like* blue best.
2 A Can I help you?
  B Yes, I *like / 'd like* an ice cream, please.
3 A What do you want to do?
  B I *like / 'd like* to play computer games.
4 A Do you want milk or orange juice?
  B I *like / 'd like* milk, please.
5 A Who's the best teacher at your school?
  B I *like / 'd like* Miss Dawes the most.
6 A Which day of the week do you like the most?
  B I *like / I' d like* Fridays.
7 A Do you want anything to eat?
  B I *like / 'd like* some chicken soup, please.
8 A What do you do in your free time?
  B I *like / 'd like* swimming and playing football.

SUMMING UP

1 Complete the mini dialogues with the missing questions.

1 A _____?
  B Yes, I'd love a dog or cat.
2 A _____?
  B No, I don't. I don't like any sports.
3 A _____?
  B Yes, I am. Very. I'd love a sandwich please.
4 A _____?
  B Yes, I do. Especially bananas and apples.
5 A _____?
  B Yes, I have. I've got a brother and two sisters.
6 A _____?
  B No, Rob hasn't got a cat but I think he's got a lizard.
7 A _____?
  B Yes, please. I'd love a glass of water. I'm really thirsty.
8 A _____?
  B No, we haven't got a car but we've all got bikes.
9 A _____?
  B Yes, I love dogs. We've got two.
10 A _____?
  B No, I haven't got a camera but I've got a smartphone.

1 | HAVING FUN

GRAMMAR
Present simple SB p.14

1 ★☆☆ (Circle) the correct option.

0   My mum *go* / *goes* to work by car.
1   He *think* / *thinks* I'm crazy.
2   Jim *look* / *looks* quite angry.
3   Dad *wash* / *washes* his car every Sunday.
4   I *doesn't* / *don't* feel very good.
5   Joe *doesn't* / *don't* want to have a shower now.
6   We *doesn't* / *don't* live very close to our school.

2 ★★☆ Rewrite the sentences. Make the positive sentences negative. Make the negative sentences positive.

0   Sally doesn't watch a lot of TV.
   Sally watches a lot of TV.
1   I like dancing.

2   Tim plays the guitar in a band.

3   Kelly doesn't miss her family a lot.

4   My parents work at the weekend.

3 ★★☆ Use the words to write questions in the present simple.

0   where / you / live?
   Where do you live?
1   you / speak / French?

2   what / your mum / do?

3   your teacher / give you / lots of homework?

4   what / bands / you / like?

5   you / play / instrument?

4 ★★☆ Match the questions in Exercise 3 with the answers below.

a   She's a businesswoman. ☐
b   Yes, I do. The piano. ☐
c   Just outside of London. ☐ 0
d   Yes, she does. Every day. ☐
e   No, I don't. ☐
f   I don't really like music. ☐

5 ★★★ Write answers to the questions in Exercise 3 so they are true for you.

0 _____
1 _____
2 _____
3 _____
4 _____
5 _____

6 ★★★ Read about Brian's hobby. Complete the text with the correct form of the words in the list.

~~not collect~~ | stand | phone | see | write | say
tell | turn | not think | not do | not play | try

My friend Brian has a really unusual hobby. He
⁰*doesn't collect* stamps and he ¹_____ the
piano. No, these are normal hobbies. Brian's hobby
is really strange. My friend Brian's hobby is being on
TV. Every time he ²_____ a TV cameraman
and presenter in town he ³_____ behind the
presenter and ⁴_____ to appear on TV.

Then he ⁵_____ me and ⁶_____ me
to watch the news on TV. So I ⁷_____ on the
TV and there he is. He ⁸_____ anything silly.
He's just there smiling. Then he ⁹_____ about
it on his blog. He ¹⁰_____ he's famous. I
¹¹_____ he's famous, just a bit crazy!

Pronunciation

Plurals and third person verb endings: /s/, /z/ or /ɪz/

Go to page 118. 🔊

like + -ing `SB p.17`

7 ★★☆ **Complete the sentences with the verbs in the list.**

~~take~~ | read | get | chat | go | do | help | tidy

Best and worst things to do on a Saturday morning.

0   I love _taking_ my dog for a walk.
1   I enjoy _____ Dad make breakfast.
2   I like _____ for a bike ride with my friends.
3   I love _____ a book in bed.
4   I enjoy _____ to my friends on the phone.
5   I hate _____ my homework.
6   I can't stand _____ up my bedroom.
7   I hate _____ out of bed before midday.

8 ★★★ **What about you? What do you like (and hate) doing on Saturday mornings? Complete the sentences so they are true for you.**

1   I love _____
2   I enjoy _____
3   I like _____
4   I hate _____
5   I can't stand _____

Adverbs of frequency `SB p.17`

9 ★☆☆ **Match the particles in the list to make adverbs of frequency and write them in the correct place.**

occasion	ten
ne	ways
rare	times
some	ally
al	ly
usu	ally
of	ver

100%	_____
↑	_____
↑	_____
↑	_____
↑	_____
↑	_____
0%	_____

10 ★★☆ **Rewrite the sentences with the adverb of frequency in the correct place.**

0   I play computer games after dinner. (usually)
   I usually play computer games after dinner.
1   You are happy. (always)
   _____
2   My best friend stays with us in the holidays. (often)
   _____
3   My mum and dad go out for a meal. (occasionally)

4   My sister is nice to me. (rarely)
   _____
5   My friends and I go to the cinema on a Saturday morning. (sometimes)
   _____
6   You are sad. (never)
   _____

11 ★★★ **Answer the questions so they are true for you.**

1   What do you always do at the weekend?
   _____
2   What do you rarely do after school?
   _____
3   What do you usually do when you're bored?
   _____
4   What do you sometimes do in the evening?
   _____
5   What do you never do on a Monday?
   _____
6   What do you often do when you're happy?
   _____

GET IT RIGHT!

Like + -ing

We use *like* + the *-ing* form of the verb. If the verb ends in consonant + *-e*, we drop the final e.
✓ *live – living*   ✗ *live – ~~liveing~~*

If a <u>short</u> verb ends in consonant + vowel + consonant, we double the final consonant before adding the *-ing*.
✓ *swim – swimming*   ✗ *swim – ~~swiming~~*

With verbs with two or more syllables, we do not usually double the final consonant.
✓ *listen – listening*   ✗ *listen – ~~listenning~~*

Correct the -ing forms.

1   writting   _____
2   comming   _____
3   studing   _____
4   waitting   _____
5   chating   _____
6   useing   _____
7   listenning   _____
8   planing   _____
9   rainning   _____
10 geting   _____

VOCABULARY

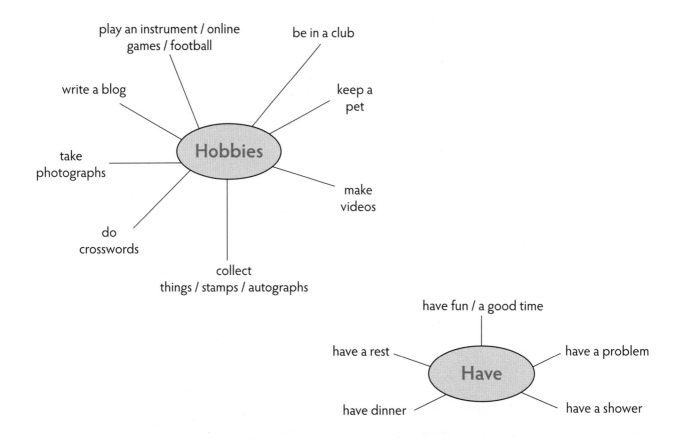

Adverbs of frequency

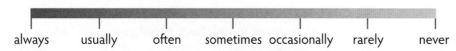

| always | usually | often | sometimes | occasionally | rarely | never |

Key words in context

have time	I never **have time** to watch TV in the morning.
have a hobby	I **have lots of hobbies** but my favourite is writing my blog.
tidy	My bedroom is very **tidy**.
busy	Sorry – I'm too **busy** to help you.
relax	My dad says that cooking the dinner helps him to **relax**.
definitely	That's **definitely** Bradley Cooper over there. I'm sure!
strange	Bird watching – that's a **strange** hobby!
smile	You never **smile** when I take your photo. You always look so sad.
positive	I feel very **positive** today. I've got a good feeling about it.
interests	My dad's got a lot of different **interests**, like reading and playing the piano.
pass the time	How do you **pass the time** when you're waiting for someone?
can't stand	Football is really, really boring. I **can't stand** it!

Hobbies `SB p.14`

1 ★☆☆ **Read the speech bubbles. Choose a word from each list and write the hobbies.**

~~write~~ | collect | be | play | take | keep

~~a blog~~ | an instrument | a pet | things
photographs | in a club

0

> It's about my life. It's about my friends and my families. It's about the things I enjoy doing (and some of the things I don't enjoy). It's about everything and anything. Read it!

write a blog

1

> I'm in a band. I'm the guitarist.
> I play for about two hours every day.

_____

2

> We meet every Friday from 7 pm to 9 pm. We learn how to do things like how to make a fire or how to cook. It's really good fun.

_____

3

> I've got about 50 teddy bears now. I've got big ones, medium-sized ones and small ones. Every time I visit a new city I always buy one.

_____

4

> It's quite hard work. Every morning I wake up early to take him for a walk and then when I get home from school I take him for another walk.

_____

5

> These are from my last holidays. We were in Corfu. It was really great. I spent hours with my camera.

_____

2 ★★☆ **Write four words that go with each verb in the boxes.**

	a team	
an orchestra	**be in**	a club
	a band	

	collect	

	write	

	play	

3 ★★★ **Use your ideas in Exercise 2 to write four sentences that are true for you.**

I'm in the school football team.
I don't collect anything.

1 _____
2 _____
3 _____
4 _____

WordWise `SB p.19`
Collocations with *have*

4 ★★☆ **Complete the sentences. Use the words in the list.**

~~shower~~ | fun | dinner | problem | rest | time

0 Do you usually have a _**shower**_ when you wake up or before you go to bed?

1 Who do you always ask for help when you have a _____ with your homework?

2 Do you always have a _____ when you feel tired?

3 What time does your family usually have _____ ?

4 Do you always have a good _____ when you're on holiday?

5 What do you do to have _____ at the weekend?

5 ★★★ **Write answers to the questions in Exercise 4 so they are true for you.**

0 _____
1 _____
2 _____
3 _____
4 _____
5 _____

READING

1 **REMEMBER AND CHECK** Complete the sentences with the names. Then check your answers in the blog on page 16 of the Student's Book.

0 _Izzy_ likes spending time with an older member of her family.

1 _____ thinks she is probably different to most young people.

2 _____ loves nature.

3 _____ is interested in what's happening in the world.

4 _____ enjoys being with other people.

5 _____ is interested in finding out about new things.

6 _____ wants to meet some famous people.

7 _____ sometimes finds her hobby very relaxing.

2 Read the text quickly. Write the names under the pictures.

1 _____

2 _____

3 _____

Gina Jones and her sister Karen have the same hobby. They both love photography. In fact, they are both in a photography club. But they don't take photographs of their friends or the interesting places they go to. They take photographs of other people taking photographs! They have a big collection of photos – more than 2,000. They write a blog about their hobby and you can see all their photos on it. The sisters don't know the people in their photos. They are just people they see in the street. But they always ask them if they can use the photos for their blog. Most people say 'yes'.

58-year-old Dan Baker loves roller coasters. Every Saturday he visits the Alton Towers theme park and spends all day on them. Luckily he lives very near to it. Some days he has more than fifty rides. His favourites are Nemesis and Th13teen. He doesn't take his wife with him – she hates roller coasters – but he often takes his grandchildren or brother. He also collects postcards of roller coasters. Every holiday he travels to theme parks in different countries; Six Flags in Mexico, PortAventura in Spain and Everland in South Korea. But Dan wants more. He wants to ride every roller coaster in the world.

Anna Roberts is a bit different to a lot of other girls. She likes animals. That's nothing strange. Many girls her age like animals. She also keeps animals as pets. There's nothing unusual about that, either. But do most girls keep spiders, lizards and snakes? Anna does. Anna has a spider from Brazil, a lizard from Australia and a snake from South Africa. She buys them from her local pet shop. She spends all her pocket money on her pets and she also spends a lot of her time looking after them. Anna knows what she wants to do when she is older. She wants to work in the insect house at a zoo.

3 Read the text again. Are sentences 1–5 'Right' (A) or 'Wrong' (B)? If there is
✳ not enough information to answer 'Right' (A) or 'Wrong' (B), choose 'Doesn't say' (C).

0 Gina and Karen put photos of their friends on their blog.   A Right   (B) Wrong   C Doesn't say

1 Some people don't want their photos on the girls' blog.   A Right   B Wrong   C Doesn't say

2 Dan Baker is married.   A Right   B Wrong   C Doesn't say

3 Dan Baker's favourite roller coaster is in America.   A Right   B Wrong   C Doesn't say

4 Anna spends five hours every day looking after her pets.   A Right   B Wrong   C Doesn't say

5 Anna wants to look after elephants at the zoo one day.   A Right   B Wrong   C Doesn't say

DEVELOPING WRITING

Routines

1 Read about Dana's hobby. Tick (✓) the photo from her blog.

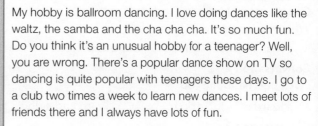

My hobby is ballroom dancing. I love doing dances like the waltz, the samba and the cha cha cha. It's so much fun. Do you think it's an unusual hobby for a teenager? Well, you are wrong. There's a popular dance show on TV so dancing is quite popular with teenagers these days. I go to a club two times a week to learn new dances. I meet lots of friends there and I always have lots of fun.

I also write a blog about dancing. It's called *Dancing with Dana*. I often take photos at the club and put them on my blog. I write something on it every day. It's a great way to meet people who have the same hobby.

2 Choose phrases from columns A, B and C to make sentences. Then check them in the text.

A	B	C
~~There's a popular dance show on TV~~	~~so~~	~~dancing is quite popular with teenagers these days.~~
I go to a club twice a week	but	learn new dances.
Maybe you think it's an unusual hobby for a teenager	and	I always have lots of fun.
I meet lots of friends there	to	you are wrong.

0 *There's a popular dance show on TV so dancing is quite popular with teenagers these days.*

1 _____

2 _____

3 _____

3 Answer the questions so they are true for you.

1 What is your hobby?

_____

2 How often do you do it?

_____

3 Where do you do it?

_____

4 Who do you do it with?

_____

5 What do you like about it?

_____

6 Is there anything you don't like about it? What?

_____

4 Use some of your ideas in Exercise 3 to complete the sentences about your hobby.

1 _____ and _____

2 _____ but _____

3 _____ so _____

4 _____ to _____

5 Write a short paragraph about your hobby (about 100–120 words). Try to use the sentences in Exercise 4.

_____

_____

_____

_____

_____

_____

_____

_____

_____

_____

_____

LISTENING

1 🔊06 **Listen to the conversations. Circle the correct answer A, B or C.**

Conversation 1
What instrument does Danny play?

A guitar   B drums   C piano

Conversation 2
What pets has Dana got?

A a lizard   B a dog   C a lizard and a dog

Conversation 3
How many stamps has Wendy got?

A 100   B 800   C 900

DIALOGUE

1 **Put the letters in order to make phrases.**

1 eb / fcalure   _____

2 twahc / tou   _____

3 ntod' / od / tath   _____

2 🔊06 **Use the phrases in Exercise 1 to complete the conversations. Then listen again and check.**

1 Thanks, but _____. It's Alfie's guitar. It's not mine.

2 No, _____. It bites.

3 _____, Mike. Don't put your glass down there.

3 **Write a short conversation for each picture. Use some of the expressions in Exercise 1.**

1 _____
_____
_____
_____
_____

2 _____
_____
_____
_____
_____

PHRASES FOR FLUENCY   SB p.19

1 **Match the words 1–6 with their meanings a–f.**

1 up to ☐
2 come on ☐
3 look out ☐
4 that's right ☐
5 hurry up ☐
6 cool ☐

a correct
b doing
c great
d let's go
e be careful
f be quick

2 **Complete the conversations with the words 1–6 from Exercise 1.**

TOM   What are you ⁰ _up to_ ?

SHONA   I'm just doing a bit of drawing.

TOM   Let's have a look.

SHONA   Here. What do you think?

TOM   Is it a picture of Jen?

SHONA   ¹ _____. What do you think?

TOM   ² _____! It's really good.

LUCY   ³ _____, Ben.

BEN   OK, OK. I'm coming. Just give me a minute.

LUCY   ⁴ _____, Ben. Run.

BEN   I am running!

LUCY   ⁵ _____. Don't run into the door. Too late!

BEN   Ow! That hurts.

Reading and Writing part 3a

1 Complete the conversations. Choose the correct answer (A, B or C).

0 Is she Spanish?
   A Yes, she does.   (B) Yes, she is.   C Yes, she isn't.

1 Can I help you?
   A Yes, she can.   B No, I don't.   C It's OK. I'm fine.

2 Hi. I'm Alex.
   A Nice to meet you.   B Yes, you are.   C I'm happy.

3 Do you like your French teacher?
   A Yes, I like them a lot. B Yes, I am.   C He's very good.

4 What would you like for lunch today?
   A Chicken and rice, please. B I like fish, please. C Yes, please.

5 Do you like dancing?
   A No, I can.   B It's OK.   C Yes, I'd love to.

Exam guide: multiple-choice replies

In the KEY Reading and Writing Part 3a you must choose the best way to reply to a statement or question. You have three possible replies to choose from.

- Read the question or statement carefully. Do you understand it? Don't look at the possible answers. How many different ways can you think of to reply? Now look at the answers. Maybe one of your ideas is there for you to choose.
- Read out the mini conversations to yourself in your head. Read the first part followed by the

first possible answer. Does it sound OK? Read the first part followed by the second possible answer. Does that sound better? Read the first part followed by the third possible answer. How does that sound? If any of them don't sound right, then cross them out immediately.

- And finally – never leave a blank answer.

2 Complete the conversations. Choose the correct answer (A, B or C).

0 Can I ask you a question, please?
   (A) Sure, what do you want to ask? B No, you can.   C Yes please.

1 What time do you wake up?
   A In the morning.   B About 7 am.   C After breakfast.

2 When do you do your homework?
   A Yes, I always do it. B I usually do it after dinner. C Sometimes.

3 How often do you go to the cinema?
   A About one time a week. B At the weekends.   C About twice a month.

4 Have you got a tablet?
   A Yes, I have got.   B Yes, I do.   C No, I haven't.

5 Hurry up.
   A Yes, please.   B I'm OK, thanks.   C OK, I'm coming.

2 MONEY AND HOW TO SPEND IT

GRAMMAR
Present continuous SB p.22

1 ★☆☆ **Complete the sentences with the names.**

Mason　Stella　Sophie
£23.50??
Dylan　Josh　Chloe

0 _Sophie_ and _Stella_ are laughing about some crazy hats.

1 _____ is looking at the TV prices.

2 _____ is buying a digital camera.

3 _____ is trying on a T-shirt.

2 ★★☆ **Complete the sentences. Use the present continuous of the verbs and the information in brackets.**

0 Adrian _isn't studying English, he's studying_
Maths. (– study English / + study Maths)

1 We _____, we _____.
(+ take the bus to school / – walk)

2 Ben and Anna _____, they
_____. (– have fun / + work on a project)

3 I _____, I _____.
(+ try to finish my homework / – take a break)

4 We _____, we _____.
(+ play computer games / – listen to music)

5 Abigail _____, she
_____. (– have lunch / + help her dad)

3 ★★☆ **Match the questions and answers.**

0 Are you having fun?　　　　 `d`

1 Is Jim in the garden?　　　　☐

2 What are you studying?　　　☐

3 Are they playing football?　 ☐

4 Am I talking too loudly?　　 ☐

5 Is he studying for the test?　☐

a Yes, he is. He's cutting the grass.

b No, they're watching a film.

c No, don't worry. It's OK.

d No, I'm not. I've got a lot of work to do for school.

e Yes, he is. He's in his room.

f French. I'm trying to remember some new words.

4 ★★★ **Complete the conversation. Use the correct form of the verbs in the list.**

~~do~~ | try | not sit | sit | laugh
run | get | try | cry | laugh

LUCY　Look at that man over there! What
0 _is_ he _doing_ ?

GAVIN　Hmm. I think he 1_____ to climb the tree.

LUCY　Oh yes, there's a cat up there. Look. It
2_____ high up in the tree.

GAVIN　Oh yes. Poor cat. What's that strange noise?
3_____ it _____

LUCY　Yeah, it's scared. Look. The man
4_____ closer to the cat.

GAVIN　But it's scared of the man too.

LUCY　Oh, no. It 5_____ to jump down.
I just hope …

GAVIN　There it goes. It's down.

LUCY　Wow. Look how fast it 6_____ now.

GAVIN　Well, I guess it's happy it 7_____ in the tree any more.

LUCY　Hey, look at those people over there. They
8_____ so the cat must be OK.

GAVIN　That's right. And you 9_____ too now!

Pronunciation
Contractions
Go to page 118. 🔊

Verbs of perception `SB p.23`

5 ★★☆ **Look at the conversations. Circle the correct options.**

0 A What do you think of this song?
   B It *sounds* / *is sounding* really cool.

1 A What are you thinking about?
   B My homework. It *looks* / *is looking* difficult.

2 A How do you like this T-shirt?
   B It *doesn't look* / *is not looking* very nice.

3 A Would you like some cake?
   B Yes, it *smells* / *is smelling* nice.

4 A Do you like the soup?
   B Yes, it *tastes* / *is tasting* wonderful.

5 A Do you like this tattoo?
   B To be honest, I think it *looks* / *is looking* awful.

6 ★★★ **Look at the examples. Write four sentences that are true for you. Use *look, sound, smell, taste* and adjectives such as *interesting, boring, cool, awful, wonderful, exciting.***

Raindrops on the window sound relaxing.
Lemon ice cream with chocolate chips tastes awful.

1 _____
2 _____
3 _____
4 _____

Present simple vs. present continuous
`SB p.25`

7 ★☆☆ **Match the pictures with the sentences.**

0 She studies English every day. **d**
1 She teaches Maths. ☐
2 She is studying for her English test. ☐
3 She is teaching Maths. ☐

8 ★★★ **Complete the email. Use the present continuous or the present simple of the verbs.**

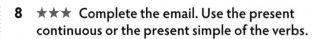

Hi Ava,

I ⁰ *'m sitting* (sit) in my room in the hotel. I really
¹_____ (like) Paris. From my window I can see
a park opposite the hotel. There aren't many people
there. There is one woman. She ²_____ (walk)
her dog. The dog ³_____ (run) after some
ducks. OK, now a man ⁴_____ (try) to help
her. I can't believe it! The dog has got the man's hat
now, and he ⁵_____ (run) away with it. The
woman ⁶_____ (shout) for the dog, but he
⁷_____ (not come) back.

How are you? What ⁸_____ (you/do)? You
always ⁹_____ (play) computer games in the
afternoon – ¹⁰_____ (you/do) it right now, too?

Love

Toby

GET IT RIGHT!
Present simple vs. present continuous

Present simple: for things that happen regularly
or that are always true.
✓ I never **do** online shopping.
✗ ~~I am never doing online shopping.~~

Present continuous: for things that are happening
at or around the time of speaking.
✓ We're **studying** English today.
✗ ~~We study English today.~~

Remember: we don't usually use verbs that describe
emotions or the way we think in the present
continuous (e.g. *think / need / like*, etc.).
✓ I **think** it's a good idea.
✗ ~~I'm thinking it's a good idea.~~

Circle **the correct options.**

Bike for sale!

I ¹*sell* / *am selling* my bike. It's 5 years old but
it ²*is looking* / *looks* new. I ³*like* / *am liking*
this bike very much, but I ⁴*want* / *am wanting*
to sell it because it's too small for me.

My name is Liam and I ⁵*am coming* / *come* to
school on my bike every day. I can show it to
you. ☺ This week I ⁶*am studying* / *study* in
room 3C. You can find me there!

VOCABULARY

It **looks** cool.

It **feels** comfortable.

It **sounds** nice.

It **tastes** good.

It **smells** awful.

newsagent's — shoe shop

chemist's — department store

Shops

bookshop — supermarket

post office

clothes shop

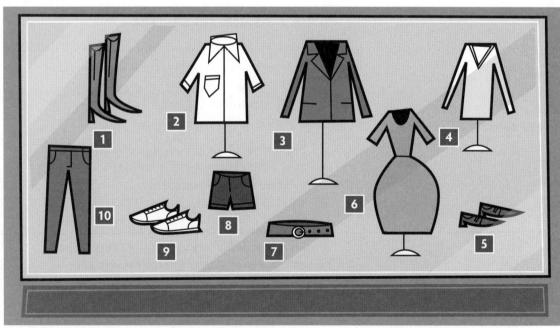

1 boots
2 shirt
3 jacket
4 jumper
5 shoes
6 dress
7 belt
8 shorts
9 trainers
10 trousers

Key words in context

customer	There aren't many **customers** in the shop right now.
size	A What **size** do you take? B Medium, please.
try on	Can I **try on** this jacket?
cost	How much does it **cost**?
spend	I don't want to **spend** so much money.
market	There are wonderful open-air **markets** in many cities.
shopping mall	Is there a **shopping mall** near here?
interested in	I'm not **interested in** designer clothes.
popular with	This shop is very **popular with** young people.
laugh at	Why are you **laughing at** me?
good-looking	Do you think he's **good-looking**?
interesting	This bookshop looks **interesting**. Let's go in.

Shops SB p.22

1 ★☆☆ **Write the names of the shops under the objects.**

0 _chemist's_

1 _____

2 _____

3 _____

4 _____

5 _____

2 ★★☆ **Complete the conversation. Use the shops from Exercise 1.**

MIA So, here's the shopping list.

LIAM OK, where do we have to go first?

MIA Let me see. Well, we need Dad's newspaper. Let's go to the 0_newsagent's_ first.

LIAM Wait a minute. What else do we need?

MIA Well, we need to buy stamps for this letter. The 1_____ isn't far. Let's go.

LIAM No, no, no. I need to get jeans first. We could start at the 2_____.

MIA Don't forget. We need to get a book for Mum first. Remember – it's her birthday soon. The 3_____ closes at 5!

LIAM Absolutely, and I need some medicine for Dad. The 4_____ isn't too far from there.

MIA OK, and there's a 5_____ where we can buy all the food we need for tonight.

3 ★★★ **Look at the sentences. Correct them so they are true for you.**

1 There's a very good shoe shop in our town. I buy all my shoes there.

_____

2 I never go to a clothes shop. I buy all my clothes on the Internet.

_____

3 There's a newsagent's in my street. I like it.

_____

Clothes SB p.24

4 ★★☆ **Write the words.**

0 btle _belt_

1 tobos _____

2 sreds _____

3 keajct _____

4 erpumj _____

5 osetsrur _____

6 hoses _____

7 rtossh _____

8 hirst _____

9 restnair _____

5 ★★☆ **Complete the text with words from Exercise 4.**

Sebastian likes black. His 0_trousers_ and his 1_____ are black, his 2_____ and his 3_____ are white, and he's wearing a grey 4_____.

6 ★★★ **Write a short text about what you are wearing today.**

_____

_____

_____

7 ★★☆ **Match the questions and answers.**

0 What do you usually wear to school? `e`

1 Do you like buying clothes? ☐

2 What's your teacher wearing today? ☐

3 Does your sister like wearing shorts? ☐

4 What do you usually wear when you're not at school? ☐

5 What do you usually wear when it's cold? ☐

a Not really. I hate shopping.

b She's wearing trousers and a jacket.

c When I'm at home, my old jumper. I love it.

d A warm coat and a hat.

e I can't choose. We all wear uniforms.

f No. She wears jeans all the time.

8 ★★★ **Choose three of the questions in Exercise 7 and write answers that are true for you.**

1 _____

2 _____

3 _____

READING

1 **Answer the questions. Then check your answers in the script on page 21 of the Student's Book.**

0 What is Tom looking for?

   A a T-shirt and some jeans   **(B)** a shirt and some trousers   **C** a T-shirt and some trousers

1 Who thinks a yellow shirt looks awful?

   A Tom   **B** Tom's parents   **C** Tom's sister

2 What does Tom think of the guy in the magazine?

   A He is very good-looking.   **B** He looks boring.   **C** His clothes are not expensive.

3 What does he think of himself?

   A He looks good in a yellow shirt.   **B** His clothes are boring.   **C** He's not good looking.

4 Who dreams of wearing fantastic clothes one day?

   A Maddy   **B** the guy in the magazine   **C** Tom

5 What does Maddy dream of?

   A ice cream   **B** being rich   **C** expensive clothes

2 **Read the web chat and match the teenagers to the photos. There is no picture for one of them.**

Buying or swapping – what's best?

Imagine you're looking around for clothes. You're in a really nice shop. You find a fantastic T-shirt and a cool jacket. Then you look at the prices and don't like the clothes any more. Just too expensive! Does this sometimes happen to you too? Then here's an idea for you. Maybe you should think about 'clothes swapping' – where you give clothes you don't want any more, and get others instead, at no cost!

1 ☐

2 ☐

A **Layla, 14**

Hi, I love swapping clothes. My friends and I sometimes meet on Saturday. We all bring one piece that we don't like any more – a T-shirt, a jumper, a pair of jeans … . Then we put all the clothes on the floor. We look at them and try them on. That's a lot of fun, and we laugh a lot. Sometimes we find something we like. Then we swap. Sometimes we don't swap.

B **Anna, 12**

I want to find something really nice at the swapping party tomorrow. A T-shirt maybe, or a jumper. My favourite colour's pink – so I'm looking for pink clothes at the moment. I've even got pink trainers, and I really like them, but they are too small for me. Maybe I can find some boots – but not in pink ;-) I often talk about clothes with my friends. I love it.

C **William, 13**

We don't say to other boys 'I really like your T-shirt!', or 'You've got cool jeans'. I think girls say these things more often. We think it's not cool to talk about clothes. But I've got a sister, Victoria. She's 16, and she sometimes helps me, and says 'This T-shirt is nice for you' or 'Don't wear brown, it's not a good colour for you.' I like that (and my friends don't know!).

3 **Read the text again. Write full sentences to answer the questions.**

0 Who has got an older sister? *William has got an older sister.*

1 Who has a lot of fun swapping clothes with her friends? _____

2 Who doesn't talk to friends about clothes? _____

3 Who likes talking to friends about clothes? _____

4 Who's going to a swapping party tomorrow? _____

5 Who wants to swap a nice pair of trainers? _____

DEVELOPING WRITING

An email to say what you're doing

1 **Read the emails. Who is writing on a mobile?**

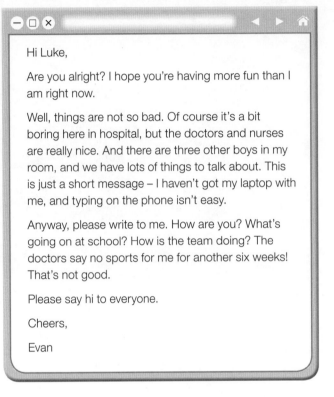

Hi Luke,

Are you alright? I hope you're having more fun than I am right now.

Well, things are not so bad. Of course it's a bit boring here in hospital, but the doctors and nurses are really nice. And there are three other boys in my room, and we have lots of things to talk about. This is just a short message – I haven't got my laptop with me, and typing on the phone isn't easy.

Anyway, please write to me. How are you? What's going on at school? How is the team doing? The doctors say no sports for me for another six weeks! That's not good.

Please say hi to everyone.

Cheers,

Evan

Hi Evelyn,

How are things with you? Hope everything's going well.

I'm with Leah and Zoe, and we're studying for the Maths test together. You know Maths is really not my favourite subject, but Leah and Zoe are really good at it. And they give me a lot of help. We're not studying right now. Leah and Zoe are playing table tennis. I'm still upstairs, but I'll join them soon.

I guess you're having a good time in London right now. You're probably walking around a street market or window shopping. Or maybe you're just buying a nice present for your sister? I'm just kidding!

By the way, we are practising for a new play at school. The first show is in two weeks' time. I hope you can come.

That's it from me. Write soon.
Lots of love,
Your sister Charlotte

2 **Mark the sentences T (true) or F (false).**

1 Evelyn's sister is in London now. ☐

2 Leah, Zoe and Charlotte are taking a break from studying. ☐

3 The three friends are playing a sport. ☐

4 Luke is visiting friends in hospital. ☐

5 The four boys in the hospital don't know what to talk about. ☐

6 Luke isn't happy that he can't play in the team for a long time. ☐

3 **Write an informal email to a friend who is on holiday in another country (about 150 words). Use the language in the Writing tip to help you.**

- Ask how your friend is.
- Tell him or her where you are and what you are doing.
- Change the subject and ask your friend a few questions about something that you are interested in.
- Say that you would like an answer as soon as possible.
- Finish with an appropriate ending.

Writing tip: informal emails

- You write informal emails to friends or family members. Your language should be informal and friendly.
- You can begin your email by asking how the other person is, for example, *How are you?*, *How are things with you?*, *Are you alright? I hope everything's well.*
- In an informal email you can use emotional expressions such as *I'm just kidding.*, *What a pain!*, *How cool is that?*, *What a shame!*
- To change the subject, you can use phrases such as *By the way, Anyway, That reminds me of …*
- You can end your email saying what you would like the other person to do, for example, *Write soon., Let me know …, Say hi to …,* and an informal ending such as *Cheers, Love, A big hug, Talk soon,* or simply *Bye bye.*

LISTENING

1 🔊09 **Listen to the conversations and complete the sentences.**

1 The boy is interested in a ⁰ _T-shirt_ .
It's £¹_____.
He thinks it's ²_____.

2 The man is interested in ³_____.
The shop assistant thinks he wants a ⁴_____.
The book is in the section ⁵_____ the man.

3 The girl wants to see a pair of ⁶_____.
She wants them in ⁷_____.
She wants to ⁸_____.

2 🔊09 **Put the conversations in order. Listen and check.**

1 BOY   OK, thanks. ☐

    BOY   Ah, OK. That's too much. ☐

    BOY   Yes. This T-shirt, how much is it? ☐

    WOMAN   Hi. Can I help you? ☐ 1

    WOMAN   Well, have a look at the T-shirts over there. They're not as pricey! ☐

    WOMAN   Let me check. Here you go … it's twenty-four pounds fifty. ☐

2 MAN   I didn't mean a recipe book. ☐

    MAN   Right. Where's that? ☐

    MAN   Hello. Have you got any books on vegetarian food? ☐

    WOMAN   Is there anything I can do for you? ☐

    WOMAN   Oh, sorry. I think you need the healthy living section. ☐

    WOMAN   Right behind you. ☐

    WOMAN   Yes, of course. That's in the section over there. There are loads of books on cooking. ☐

3 GIRL   Yes, have you got these jeans in grey? ☐

    GIRL   Thank you. Can I try them on please? ☐

    GIRL   Um … 8. ☐

    MAN   Just a moment. Here you are. ☐

    MAN   Let me look … What size do you take? ☐

    MAN   Of course. The changing rooms are over there, on your right. ☐

    MAN   Hello. Can I help? ☐

▰▰▰ TRAIN TO THiNK ▰▰▰

Exploring numbers

1 **Read the text. Can you work out how Logan finds the answer to the teacher's questions so fast? Check with the answer at the bottom of the page.**

> **Note:**
> Even numbers:
> 2 4 6 8 …
> Odd numbers:
> 1 3 5 7 …

Logan is brilliant at Maths. One day, his Maths teacher asks the class how quickly they can find the sum of the first 50 odd numbers. The other kids are starting to think when Logan calls out, '2,500'! The teacher thinks that Logan was just lucky. 'OK,' she says, 'let's make it a bit more difficult. Who's fastest at finding the sum of the first 75 odd numbers?' Everybody is thinking hard. Fifteen seconds later, Logan calls out, '5,625'! He's right again. The teacher is puzzled. How does Logan do it?

2 **A question for you: What's the sum of the first 66 odd numbers?**

_____

Answer
It's easy to calculate the sum of a series of consecutive odd numbers that start with 1. Look!
What's the sum of the first three odd numbers? Easy! Just multiply 3 x 3. The answer: 9!
What's the sum of the first nine odd numbers? Again, not difficult. Just multiply 9 x 9!
So to get the sum of the first 50 odd numbers you have to multiply 50 x 50, etc.

Listening part 1

1 🔊 10 You will hear three short conversations. There is one question for each conversation. For each question tick (✓) A, B or C.

1 What number is Keith's house?

☐ A ☐ B ☐ C

2 What time does Tim's school start?

☐ A ☐ B ☐ C

3 Which picture shows what's in Dawn's bag?

☐ A ☐ B ☐ C

Exam guide: multiple-choice pictures

In a multiple-choice picture task, you hear short conversations and then have to choose the correct picture to answer a simple question.

- Before you listen, look at the pictures. What words do you expect to hear? These are the words you need to listen out for.
- If the pictures show numbers or times, practise saying them to yourself in your head before you listen.
- Be careful not to tick the first picture you hear. Often, you will hear all three pictures mentioned. You need to listen carefully to select the right one.
- Listen carefully to the whole conversation. The correct answer is often only revealed at the end.
- Don't worry if you don't get the answer the first time you listen. You will hear each conversation twice.
- If you get the answer on the first listening, use the second time to check the answer.
- Always choose an answer even if you have no idea which one is correct.

2 🔊 11 You will hear five short conversations. There is one question for each conversation. For each question tick (✓) A, B or C.

1 What's the weather like?

☐ A ☐ B ☐ C

2 Which is Anne's dog?

☐ A ☐ B ☐ C

3 Where is Marco from?

Portugal   Chile   Brazil

☐ A ☐ B ☐ C

4 How far is Jasmine's house from her school?

☐ A ☐ B ☐ C

5 What is Frank's favourite sport?

☐ A ☐ B ☐ C

CONSOLIDATION

LISTENING

1 🔊 12 **Listen to Annie talking about her hobby. Which of these items has she got in her collection?**

2 🔊 12 **Listen again. Answer the questions.**

0 What is Annie's hobby and how is it different from other teenagers'?
She shops for clothes. It's different because she collects old clothes from the 1940s.

1 Who buys the clothes that Annie wears every day?

2 Where does Annie buy the things for her hobby?

3 Why is her collection quite small?

4 Where does she keep her collection?

5 Why doesn't she wear these clothes?

VOCABULARY

3 **Unscramble the words in *italics*.**

0 Can you go to the *rapumkerest* and get some milk?
supermarket

1 If you're cold, then put on a *premuj*. _____

2 I'm going to the *stop cofefi* so I can get you some stamps. _____

3 Mum, I need some new *reatrins*. These have got holes in them. _____

4 The new *prentatmed toser* is really big. You can buy anything there. _____

5 Put some *hostrs* on. It's really hot today.

_____

6 If your hands are cold, put on your *levsog*.

_____

7 My mum's a doctor. She works at the local *sopithal*.

_____

GRAMMAR

4 **Rewrite the sentences to include the words in brackets.**

0 I get up late on Saturday mornings. (never)
I never get up late on Saturday mornings.

1 Dad's in the bath again. (singing)

_____

2 That sounds a great idea. (like)

_____

3 My dog runs after birds in the park. (always)

_____

4 Polly like hot food but she's eating your curry. (doesn't)

_____

5 Mum cooks at the weekend. (usually)

_____

6 Why are you drinking the coffee? It awful. (tastes)

_____

7 I like music but I'm enjoying listening to this! (not)

_____

8 I go swimming on Sunday mornings. (sometimes)

_____

9 My mum likes most fruit she doesn't like apples. (but)

_____

10 James loves this band but he isn't the concert. (enjoying)

_____

5 Complete the text with the present simple or present continuous form of the verbs in brackets.

Hi Archie,

I'm in Rome and I ⁰**_'m having_** (have) a great holiday. It's a wonderful place. At the moment I ¹_____ (sit) in a café with Jennie and I ²_____ (write) you a postcard. We ³_____ (eat) a pizza and it ⁴_____ (taste) amazing. We ⁵_____ (watch) the Italian people in the street. The people ⁶_____ (wear) really beautiful clothes here in Italy and they ⁷_____ (look) so cool. Talking of cool – all the teenagers ⁸_____ (ride) Vespas here – you know, those really great motorbikes. But they ⁹_____ (make) a lot of noise. They ¹⁰_____ (sound) like big mosquitoes.

Anyway, bye for now. The waiter ¹¹_____ (walk) over to our table with our ice cream!

DIALOGUE

6 Complete the conversation with the words in the list.

~~on~~ | problem | much | making | looks
cool | up | careful | do | right

BEN Come ⁰___*on*___, Sue. Stop looking at the shoes.

SUE But they're really ¹_____.

BEN But we're here to buy George a present. Remember?

SUE Because it's his birthday tomorrow.

BEN That's ²_____. Now, he really likes ³_____ models so …

SUE What about this ship?

BEN Interesting. How ⁴_____ is it?

SUE £200.

BEN What! We've only got £10.

SUE Oh. So let's forget the ship, then.

BEN Hey, that aeroplane ⁵_____ good.

SUE What are you ⁶_____ to, Ben?

BEN I'm just getting this aeroplane off the shelf.

SUE Ben – don't ⁷_____ that.

BEN It's OK. Don't worry.

SUE Be ⁸_____.

(CRASH!)

SUE Oh, too late. I think we've got a ⁹_____!

READING

7 Read the text about Dan. Mark the sentences T (true) or F (false).

I've got quite an unusual hobby for a teenager. My hobby is bird watching. Some of my friends think it's a silly hobby but they don't really understand what it's all about.

I love bird watching because I get to spend a lot of time out of the house. Many teens spend most of their time indoors playing on their tablets or watching TV. I like doing that too, but not all day. I like walking in the countryside and seeing what I can find. There's always a surprise or two. I usually go bird watching at the weekend, for three or four hours in the afternoon. I sometimes go for an hour really early in the morning before school. It's the best time to see birds.

I keep a list of all the birds I see. There are more than 250 birds on it. That's most of the birds that live in the UK, but there are still a few more to see.

But the best thing about my hobby is that it doesn't cost much money. I've got a pair of binoculars – a present from my granddad – and a few books. I only need these things. Everything else is free.

0 All of Dan's friends think his hobby is great. [F]

1 Dan doesn't like playing computer games. [ ]

2 Dan always sees something different when he goes for a walk. [ ]

3 The best time to see birds is after lunch on a Saturday or Sunday. [ ]

4 Dan writes down all the birds that he sees. [ ]

5 You don't need any money to be a birdwatcher. [ ]

WRITING

8 Write a short text about your hobby (120–150 words). Include this information.

- What it is.
- When and where you do it.
- How much money you spend on it.
- Why you like doing it.

3 FOOD FOR LIFE

GRAMMAR
Countable and uncountable nouns SB p.32

1 ★☆☆ (Circle) the correct words.

0 The books *is* / (*are*) on my desk.
1 The milk *is* / *are* in the kitchen.
2 There *is* / *are* three English lessons this week.
3 The cheese *is* / *are* old.
4 These apples *is* / *are* very good!
5 It *is* / *are* six o'clock.
6 My homework tonight *is* / *are* easy.
7 There *is* / *are* water on the floor.

2a ★☆☆ Write the words from Exercise 1 in the correct columns.

~~book~~ | ~~water~~ | cheese | homework
lesson | milk | time | apple

Countable		Uncountable	
0	book	0	water
1		7	
2		8	
3		9	
4		10	
5		11	
6		12	

2b ★☆☆ Now write these words in the correct columns.

butter | computer | juice | potato | shirt | pencil

a / an / some / any SB p.32

3 ★☆☆ Complete the sentences with *a / an* or *some*.

0 I'd like ___some___ strawberries, please.
1 We've got _____ lesson at 10 o'clock.
2 There are _____ apples in the kitchen.
3 This is _____ old computer.
4 Let's make _____ orange juice.
5 I'd like _____ cheese sandwich, please.
6 Can I have _____ water, please?
7 You've got _____ nice shirts!

4 ★★☆ Complete the conversation with *some* or *any*.

DAD It's Mum's birthday tomorrow. Let's make a cake for her.
ALEX Yeah, great idea. What do we need?
DAD Well, first we need ⁰ ___some___ sugar and ¹_____ butter.
ALEX What about fruit?
DAD We're going to make a banana cake, so we need ²_____ bananas.
ALEX OK. But we've got ³_____ oranges and strawberries here as well. Can we use them, too?
DAD Well, maybe we can put ⁴_____ strawberries on the top of the cake, but I'm sure we don't need ⁵_____ oranges. It's a banana cake, Alex!
ALEX OK. Oh, it's going to be a great cake, Dad. But don't forget the candles. A birthday cake isn't right if there aren't ⁶_____ candles on it.
DAD That's right.
ALEX So, can we please put ⁷_____ candles on it?
DAD Sure. Now – what do we do first?
ALEX I can look on the computer to get ⁸_____ information about cakes. OK?
DAD No, we haven't got ⁹_____ time for that. Come on – let's start.

(how) much / (how) many / a lot of / lots of SB p.32

5 ★★★ Complete the sentences with *much* or *many*.

0 How ___many___ desks are there in your classroom?
1 My school hasn't got _____ computers.
2 How _____ butter do we need?
3 I haven't got _____ friends.
4 I haven't got _____ time before dinner.
5 How _____ legs has a spider got?
6 How _____ ice cream is there in the fridge?
7 We haven't got _____ homework tonight.

6 ★★☆ Replace *a lot of* with *much* or *many*.

0 I haven't got ~~a lot of~~ friends. _*many*_

1 There aren't a lot of people here. _____

2 There isn't a lot of sugar in my coffee. _____

3 We haven't got a lot of time. _____

4 Please don't buy a lot of cheese. _____

5 There aren't a lot of songs on this CD. _____

6 Hundreds of people went to the concert, but there weren't a lot of teenagers. _____

7 There isn't a lot of information in this book.

_____

too many / *too much* / *not enough* + noun SB p.35

7 ★☆☆ Complete the sentences with the words in the list.

~~too much traffic~~ | a lot of traffic | a lot of clothes
a lot of people | too many people | too many clothes

0 I can't cross the road – there's
   *too much traffic* !

1 I've got
   _____ .
   I think I'll throw some old ones away.

2 I can't get on the bus – there are

   _____
   on it!

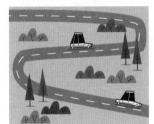

3 We'll get there easily – there isn't

   _____
   today!

4 I bought

   _____
   yesterday.

5 I was really happy because

   _____
   came to my party.

8 ★★☆ Circle the correct words.

0 I can't go out tonight – *I haven't got enough /* (*I've got too much*) *homework* to do.

1 Let's do it later. *There isn't enough / There's too much* time now.

2 We need to go shopping; *there isn't enough / there's too much* food for tonight.

3 We can't sit down because *there aren't enough / there are too many* chairs.

4 I need to tidy my room – *there aren't enough / there are too many* things on the floor!

too + adjective, (*not*) + adjective + *enough* SB p.35

9 ★★☆ Complete the sentences with a phrase from the list.

~~not tired enough~~ | too tired | too old
too warm | not warm enough | not old enough

0 I can't go to sleep – I'm _*not tired enough*_ .

1 Sorry, you're only 12. You're _____
   to see this film.

2 Sorry, I'm _____ to go out tonight!
   I just want to go to bed!

3 What? Go for a swim in the sea? Sorry, no, the water's _____ .

4 I don't want to go for a walk. It's a very sunny day, so it's _____ to walk.

GET IT RIGHT! 👁

a lot of / *lots of*

We use *of* + noun after *a lot* and *lots*.

✓ *There are **a lot of** fast food restaurants in my town.*

✗ *There are ~~a lot~~ fast food restaurants in my town.*

✓ *We've got **lots of** money.*

✗ *We've got ~~lots~~ money.*

We use *a* + *lot* + *of* but *lots of*.

✓ *There are **a lot of** / **lots of** people at the party.*

✗ *There are ~~a lots of~~ people at the party.*

Correct the sentences.

0 There is lots food to eat.
   *There is lots of food to eat.*

1 We have alot of sandwiches and a lots of sausages.

   _____

2 We don't have much of water.

   _____

3 There aren't a lot places to park the car.

   _____

4 Jo buys lots cakes and a lot ice cream.

VOCABULARY

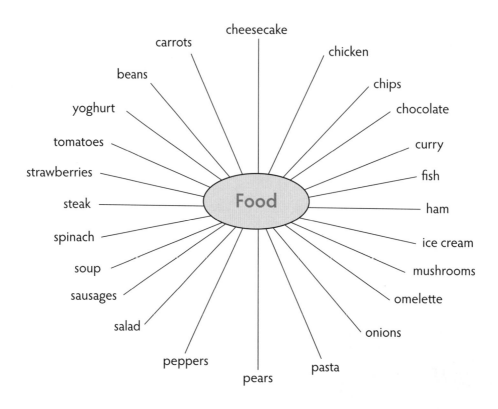

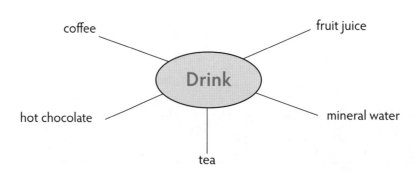

Words that go together

roast chicken
boiled potatoes
grilled fish
fried mushrooms
ham and cheese omelette
vanilla and chocolate ice cream
mixed salad
pasta with tomato sauce

Describing food

delicious
disgusting
fatty
fresh
horrible
salty
spicy
sweet
tasty
yummy

Expressions with *have got*

have got an idea
have got a headache
have got time
have got something to do
have got a problem

Food and drink SB p.32

1 ★☆☆ **Complete the puzzle. What is the 'mystery' word in the middle?**

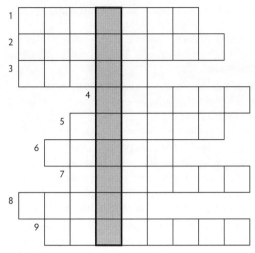

The mystery word is _____.

Adjectives to talk about food SB p.35

2 ★★★ Circle **the word that does not follow the adjective.**

0	roast	**a** chicken	**b** potatoes	**c** strawberries
1	grilled	**a** soup	**b** fish	**c** sausages
2	boiled	**a** carrots	**b** potatoes	**c** salad
3	fried	**a** curry	**b** chicken	**c** onions
4	mixed	**a** salad	**b** vegetables	**c** chicken
5	hot	**a** water	**b** fruit juice	**c** chocolate

3 ★☆☆ **Complete the adjectives. Then check in the word list 'Describing food'.**

0 de _l_ icious

1 di __ gu __ __ in __   5 s __ __ t __

2 fa __ __ y   6 s __ __ cy

3 fr __ __ h   7 s __ ee __

4 ho __ __ ib __ __   8 ta __ __ y

4 ★★☆ **Look at the words in Exercise 3. Match them to the definitions.**

0 it has a very nice taste (2 words) _delicious, tasty_

1 it has a very bad taste (2 words) _____

2 it has a lot of fat in it _____

3 it has sugar in it _____

4 it has a hot and strong taste (for example, curry)

_____

5 it is in a natural condition (not from a tin or frozen)

_____

5 ★★☆ **Invent two dishes, one that you think is really delicious, and one that you think is really disgusting.**

Example:

Delicious — chicken curry with mushrooms and chips

Disgusting — vanilla ice cream with spinach and chips

WordWise SB p.37

Expressions with *have got*

6 ★☆☆ **Match the sentences and the pictures.**

a I've got an idea!

b I've got a headache.

c I haven't got time.

d I've got something to do.

7 ★★☆ **Match the sentences to a–d in Exercise 6.**

0	'Let's go to the cinema.'	a
1	'I'm taking aspirin.'	
2	'And I'm going to do it now!'	
3	'Let's play tomorrow, OK?'	

READING

1 **REMEMBER AND CHECK** Match the statements and the food. Then check your answers in the article on page 31 of the Student's Book.

0   In Japan, they are sometimes square. `c`

1   They have more sugar in them than strawberries. ☐

2   It has a lot of vitamins that are good for the skin and hair. ☐

3   They help the body produce a chemical called 'serotonin'. ☐

4   A lot of people think they're vegetables, but they're fruit. ☐

a   bananas
b   avocados
c   watermelons
d   honey
e   lemons

2 Read the text. Match the photographs and the countries.

grasshopper **1** ☐

kudu **2** ☐

rattlesnake **3** ☐

chicken **4** ☐

guinea pig **5** ☐

chips in curry sauce **6** ☐

a   the USA
b   Peru
c   Brazil
d   Britain
e   South Africa
f   Mexico

Different food around the world

It is fantastic to go to different countries. You can see wonderful places and visit great cities. You can go to museums and markets, and meet people with different ideas and a different language. And, of course, you can eat different food, too.

Sometimes the food in another country is different because it has a different taste – for example, food in India is often very spicy. But sometimes it is because the food itself is very different. So, what things do people eat in other countries that perhaps you don't eat in yours?

Well, in Mexico, some people really like to eat grasshoppers. Do you think that's strange? Perhaps, but of course the people who eat grasshoppers don't think so, and in fact grasshoppers are very good for you.

If you go to South Africa, you see that some places serve kudu – it's a kind of big antelope. And in some parts of the USA, you can eat rattlesnake – some people say it tastes like chicken, but other people say it's like fish. A lot of people just say: 'It's delicious!'

Talking of chicken, grilled chicken hearts are a big favourite in Brazil. People eat them with meat and rice at barbecues. Finally, if you go to a restaurant in some parts of Peru, it's possible that you will see fried guinea pig on the menu. It's a very important food for many people in the mountain parts of the country.

So perhaps you are thinking: 'Oh, no, please – I just want to eat chips!' Oh, yes, chips (or 'fries' in the USA). Now they're the same in every country, right? Wrong! In many places in Britain, people eat their chips with a curry sauce!

So, when you eat a meal, stop and think. Perhaps people from other countries think that your food is really strange!

3 Mark the sentences T (true) or F (false). Correct the false ones.

0   Food in India is sometimes very spicy. `T`

1   Some people eat grasshoppers in Mexico. ☐
_____

2   Grasshoppers are good for you. ☐
_____

3   Everyone thinks rattlesnake tastes like chicken. ☐
_____

4   In Brazil, some people eat fried chicken hearts. ☐
_____

5   Guinea pig is an important food everywhere in Peru. ☐

6   Chips (or fries) are the same in every country. ☐

7   In Britain, some people eat chips with curry sauce. ☐
_____

DEVELOPING WRITING

A recipe

1 Read the recipe for Bolognese sauce. About how long does it take to make this sauce?

frying pan

minced beef

Bolognese sauce

What you need (the ingredients):

1 tbsp olive oil
1 small carrot, cut into small pieces
1 small onion, cut into small pieces
400g can of tomatoes
some fresh basil leaves
250g minced beef
400g spaghetti
25g toasted breadcrumbs

How to make it:

1 Heat the oil in a frying pan. Put in the carrot and onion and cook for 5 minutes.

2 Add the minced beef to the carrot and onion. Cook for a few minutes (until the meat is brown).

3 Put the tomatoes into the frying pan, and cook for another 5 minutes. Stir all the time.

4 Add the basil leaves, then cook slowly for 15 minutes.

5 Cook the spaghetti. (Usually eight to ten minutes.)

6 Put the spaghetti on a plate. Put the sauce on top of the spaghetti. Put some basil leaves on top and the breadcrumbs.

2 Read the recipe again. Answer the questions.

1 How long do you cook the carrot and onion?

_____

2 When is the meat OK?

_____

3 How long does it take to cook the spaghetti?

_____

4 What do you put on top of the sauce?

_____

3 a Read the section 'How to make it' again. Match the verbs and the definitions.

1 heat ☐
2 add ☐
3 stir ☐

a put one thing together with another thing
b move round and round (often with a spoon)
c make something hot

3 b Tick (✓) the correct option.

All the verbs are in:
the present tense ☐
the imperative ☐
the past tense ☐

Writing tip: a recipe

- Choose the dish. Something simple is a good idea! (A chocolate cake? Chips? An omelette? …)
- Think of all the things you need (the ingredients). Write them down. Use a dictionary to help you with words you don't know.
- Think of any things you need to do to the ingredients before you start cooking (e.g. cut / chop / dice / …) Write the words down.
- Think of the steps ('How to make it'). What are the verbs you need? Write them down. Use a dictionary to help you with words you don't know.

4 Write a recipe for something that you know how to make or cook.

LISTENING

1 🔊 13 **Listen to the conversation between Sally and Maggie. Tick (✓) the things that Sally puts in her dish.**

beans	☐	carrots	☐
chicken	☐	chilli pepper	☐
garlic	☐	meat	☐
mushrooms	☐	onion	☐
potatoes	☐	red pepper	☐
tomato	☐		

2 🔊 13 **Listen again. Mark the sentences T (true) or F (false).**

0 Sally is cooking something for dinner. **T**

1 Sally's got an idea for a new kind of food. ☐

2 The onions, tomatoes and red peppers are grilled together. ☐

3 Sally's dish isn't spicy. ☐

4 Sally uses fried steak. ☐

5 They can eat Sally's food with salad and potatoes. ☐

6 Maggie thinks *chilli con carne* is from Mexico. ☐

7 *Chilli con carne* usually has mushrooms in it. ☐

DIALOGUE

1 **Put the words in order to make phrases.**

0 OK / It's. _____ *It's OK.* _____

1 sorry / I'm / really _____

2 really / I / bad / feel _____

3 it / worry / Don't / about _____

2 **Use the phrases in Exercise 1 to complete the conversation. There may be more than one possible answer.**

A Jacky? Do you remember that I borrowed your book?

B Yes, I remember. Why?

A Well – I can't find it. I haven't got it any more.
   0_____ *I'm really sorry* _____.

B Oh, 1_____, Brian. It's not a very good book!

A 2_____, Jacky. I want to buy another one for you.

B No, Brian. 3_____. Really. Look – I've got an idea.

A What?

B There's a film of the book now. It's at the cinema this weekend. Take me to see it!

A Oh, OK then.

PHRASES FOR FLUENCY SB p.37

1 **Put the sentences in the correct order.**

1	A	Hey, Fatima. I've got some news.
☐	A	Well, they're from Italy. They're going to be here for a couple of weeks.
☐	B	Oh really? What is it?
☐	A	Some friends are coming next week to visit me.
☐	B	So what?
☐	B	Great. I love parties!
☐	A	Oh, I'm sorry, Fatima, I didn't mean to. Of course I want you to come as well.
☐	B	What about me? Don't forget me!
☐	B	OK. Some Italians here in our town! That's good news.
☐	A	Yes, it is. I want to have a party when they're here.
☐	A	Me too! I'm going to invite Joe, and Garry, and June, and Melinda, and … .

2 **Complete the conversations with the words in the list.**

~~Actually~~ | What about me | So what
I didn't mean to | as well | a couple of

1 A Do you like this curry?

   B Yes, it's delicious. 0_ *Actually* _, curry's my favourite food, I think. But I like other things 1_____, of course.

2 A I'm going to the cinema with 2_____ friends.

   B 3_____? Can I come too?

3 A John's very angry with you.

   B 4_____? I don't like him anyway.

4 A Katie? Did I say something wrong?

   B Yes. And it hurt me!

   A Well, I'm really sorry. 5_____.

Pronunciation

Vowel sounds: /ɪ/ and /iː/
Go to page 118. 🔊

CAMBRIDGE ENGLISH: Key

Reading and Writing part 3b

1 Complete the conversation between Jack and his dad. For each space 1–5, choose one of the sentences A–H.

JACK   What's for dinner tonight, Dad?

DAD   0   _C_

JACK   Again? We had that on Monday night.

DAD   1 _____

JACK   Oh well, that's OK. I really like fish and chips. Can we have some peas too?

DAD   2 _____

JACK   Actually, they're in the cupboard, not the fridge.

DAD   3 _____

JACK   Sure. Here you are. Do you need any more help?

DAD   4 _____

JACK   Yes, it is. Is that why you cook it all the time?

DAD   5 _____

JACK   Yes, you're right. Sorry, Dad!

A   No, thanks. Cooking fish and chips is easy!

B   Can you get them for me?

C   Fish and chips.

D   We haven't got any.

E   That's not true. Sometimes I make curry.

F   I know. And we're having it again tonight.

G   I don't need any help, thanks.

H   OK. I think we've got some in the fridge.

2 Complete the conversation between a waiter and a customer. For each space 1–5, choose one of the sentences A–H.

CUSTOMER   Can I have the menu, please?

WAITER   0   _C_

CUSTOMER   Thanks. I think I'd like the mushrooms to start. Are they fresh?

WAITER   1 _____

CUSTOMER   Good, I'll have the mushrooms then.

WAITER   2 _____

CUSTOMER   The chicken, please.

WAITER   3 _____

CUSTOMER   No problem. OK, I'll have the fish, please.

WAITER   4 _____

CUSTOMER   Oh, grilled, please. And some rice and beans.

WAITER   5 _____

CUSTOMER   Just some water, please.

A   We haven't got fresh mushrooms.

B   Thank you. Would you like some water too?

C   Yes, of course. Here it is.

D   Yes, they are, Madam.

E   Of course. Would you like it grilled or fried?

F   I'm very sorry, Madam – we haven't got any chicken today.

G   Thank you, Madam. And to drink?

H   Very good, Madam. And for the main course?

Exam guide: dialogue matching

In this exercise, you read a conversation and choose a sentence to go in each of the empty spaces.

- You choose five sentences (one is given to you) from eight possibilities. This means you have to be careful not to choose sentences that are wrong.
- Remember that some of the 'wrong' answers are almost right.
- When you choose a sentence for a space, make sure it works for what is said before it, and also what is said after it. For example, look at space number 2 above. Jack says: 'Can we have some peas too?' A possible answer is D: 'We haven't got any.' BUT – and this is important – Jack then says: 'Actually, they're in the cupboard … '. So D cannot be correct. The correct answer is H. (Another example: why is 'G' NOT the right answer for space 4?)
- When you finish choosing the sentences, read through the complete conversation again to check your answers. Does the conversation make sense?

4 | FAMILY TIES

GRAMMAR

Possessive adjectives and pronouns
SB p.40

1 ★☆☆ (Circle) the correct words.

⁰I / (My) family is quite big. There are ¹I / my three sisters Vicky, Mila and Madison, and there are ²us / our brothers Dylan and Isaac. And ³I / my name's Ryan, so we are three boys and three girls. ⁴Us / Our sisters love playing football for the school team. ⁵They / Their team is really good. Vicky is ⁶they / their goalkeeper. ⁷She / Her friends think she's the best goalkeeper in the world. ⁸Us / Our mum and dad love football too, so on Sundays we all go and watch the three girls play. Dad's got a brother. ⁹He / His name's Jonathan. He sometimes goes with us to watch the girls play. Uncle Jonathan often says to me, ¹⁰'You / Your sisters are good footballers, but I'm sure you are better.' I think that's funny.

2 ★★☆ Rewrite the sentences using possessive pronouns.

0 Is this your dog? *Is this dog yours?*

1 Is that his car? _____

2 Are these your jeans? _____

3 Is this my sandwich? _____

4 Are these our books? _____

5 Is that her house? _____

Whose and possessive 's SB p.40

3 ★☆☆ Look at the example. Write sentences in the same style. In each sentence, put the apostrophe in the right position.

0 A Whose is this pen?
  B It's his. (Peter) *I think it's Peter's.*

1 A Whose are those shoes?
  B They're theirs. (my friends) _____

2 A Is this your car?
  B No, it's hers. (Mrs Miller) _____

3 A Are those your brothers' bikes?
  B No, they're theirs. (my sisters) _____

4 A Is this John's phone?
  B No, it's his. (Tom) _____

5 A Whose are these keys?
  B They're hers. (Sandra) _____

4 ★★☆ (Circle) the correct words.

0 A Can you check (who's) / whose at the door?
  B It's (Peter's) / Peter friend, Henry.

1 A Who's / Whose car is this?
  B It's the Miller's / Millers' new car.

2 A Is it Sam / Sam's bike?
  B No, it's his sister Barbara / Barbara's.

3 A Our teacher's / teachers son is a doctor.
  B You mean Mrs Smith's / Smith son?

4 A Who's / Whose your favourite band?
  B I really like The Arctic Monkey's / Monkeys' songs a lot.

5 A Who's / Whose are these books?
  B They aren't mine. I think they're James / James's.

5 ★★★ Complete the conversations.

1 A I really like ⁰ _your_ jacket, Bob. It looks really good on ¹_____.
  B ²_____ isn't ³_____. It's Kev's. He lent it to ⁴_____. I've got to give it back to ⁵_____ later.

2 A Do you know the Richard twins? ⁶_____ live next to Sally. In fact she lives at number 9, and ⁷_____ house is number 11.
  B Yes, I know Sally. My sister is a good friend of ⁸_____. She's a friend of mine too.

3 A I'm sure that's Liam's dog over there. So where is ⁹_____? He never goes anywhere without ¹⁰_____ dog.
  B It's not ¹¹_____. Liam's dog is black and that one is brown.

4 A Hey, what are ¹²_____ doing, Henry? That's ¹³_____ sandwich. It's not ¹⁴_____!
  B I'm sorry. ¹⁵_____ was hungry. Here ¹⁶_____ are. Don't be angry with ¹⁷_____, OK?

5 A ¹⁸_____ is this camera?
  B Let's ask Joseph. I think it's ¹⁹_____. Or talk to Rebecca. Maybe it's ²⁰_____.

Pronunciation

-er /ə/ at the end of words
Go to page 119. 🔊

was / were `SB p.43`

6 ★☆☆ (Circle) the correct option.

0 Breakfast this morning (was) / were delicious, but the bananas wasn't / (weren't) very sweet.

1 Mrs Donald, our English teacher, was / were really cool yesterday. We was / were happy too.

2 My parents wasn't / weren't at home yesterday evening. They was / were at my school with my teacher.

3 I was / were really hungry but there wasn't / weren't any sandwiches left.

4 The film was / were really boring. We wasn't / weren't very interested in it.

5 They was / were very late. There wasn't / weren't many people left at the party.

7 ★☆☆ Complete the sentences with was or were.

0 A ___Was___ it cold this morning?
   B Cold? Not really.

1 A _____ David and Daniel born in the same year?
   B No. David is 9, Daniel is 11.

2 A _____ your parents angry with you?
   B Not at all.

3 A _____ all your friends at your party?
   B Only Tony wasn't. He was ill.

4 A _____ she hungry?
   B Yes, very, very hungry.

5 A _____ they at home?
   B No, they _____ still at school.

8 ★★☆ Complete the dialogue between a police officer (PO) and Eric with was, wasn't, were or weren't.

PO So, just let me check your story again.
ERIC Sure.
PO Your mum and dad ⁰ ___were___ in the garden.
ERIC Yes, they ¹_____. They ²_____ very happy.
PO And your brother ³_____ in the garden too.
ERIC No, he ⁴_____. He ⁵_____ in the garage. He ⁶_____ very happy. In fact, he ⁷_____ very angry.
PO And ⁸_____ your sister, Jill, in the house?

ERIC Yes, she ⁹_____. She ¹⁰_____ in the kitchen. She ¹¹_____ very hungry.
PO And the twins? ¹²_____ they in the kitchen with her?
ERIC No, they ¹³_____. They ¹⁴_____ in the living room – in front of the TV.
PO And you, Eric. Where ¹⁵_____ you?
ERIC I ¹⁶_____ tired and I ¹⁷_____ very well. I ¹⁸_____ in bed.
PO Sleeping.
ERIC Yes, I ¹⁹_____ asleep.
PO So, if you ²⁰_____ asleep, how do you know where everyone was?

9 ★★☆ Answer the questions so they are true for you.

1 Were you at school yesterday at 3 pm?
_____

2 Was it hot yesterday?
_____

3 Was your teacher happy this morning?
_____

4 Were you in bed early last night?
_____

5 Were you late to school last week?
_____

6 Was your best friend happy to see you this morning?
_____

GET IT RIGHT! 👁

it's and its

We use *it's* as a short form of *it is*. We always use an apostrophe (') between *it* and the *-s*.

✓ *It's my mum's birthday today.*
✗ ~~Its my mum's birthday today.~~

We use *its* to talk about possession when the subject is an object or an animal*. *Its* never has an apostrophe.

✓ *This book's very old. **Its** pages are yellow.*
✗ *This book's very old. ~~It's pages~~ are yellow.*

*We sometimes use *his/her* to talk about animals that are our pets.

Put four apostrophes (') in the correct place.

I love my new mobile phone. I love the colour. Its red. Its my favourite colour. The screen is big and the camera takes good pictures. My sister loves her phone because of its modern design and its apps and because its small. Her friends gave it to her for her birthday. Its really nice, but I think mine is the best.

VOCABULARY

Family members

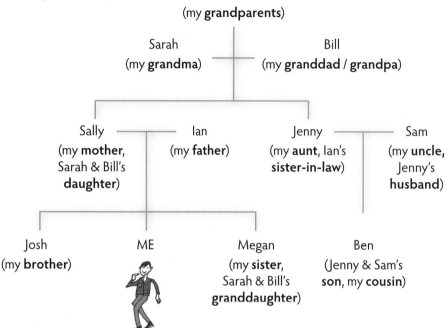

(my **grandparents**)

Sarah
(my **grandma**)

Bill
(my **granddad / grandpa**)

Sally
(my **mother**,
Sarah & Bill's
daughter)

Ian
(my **father**)

Jenny
(my **aunt**, Ian's
sister-in-law)

Sam
(my **uncle**,
Jenny's
husband)

Josh
(my **brother**)

ME

Megan
(my **sister**,
Sarah & Bill's
granddaughter)

Ben
(Jenny & Sam's
son, my **cousin**)

Possessive adjectives and pronouns

Possessive adjectives	Possessive pronouns
my	mine
your	yours
his	his
her	hers
its	–
our	ours
their	theirs

Key words in context

side of the family	Here's a photo of my dad's **side of the family**.
fight	They are three brothers and they **fight** quite a lot.
spend time	Do you **spend** a lot of **time** with your family?
hero	Miya and Tiffany are **heroes** – they saved their father's life.
ambulance	Let's call the **ambulance**. Quick!
disappear	David **disappears** under the water.
in trouble	I think they're **in trouble**. Let's help them.
open presents	Can we **open** our **presents** now?
watch a performance	Let's **watch the 6 pm performance**.
international	When is **International** Children's Day?
national	Today is a **national** holiday in Turkey.
share	Let's **share** the pizza. It's big enough.
together	It's good for children and parents to have time to spend **together**.
invitation	Thanks for the **invitation** to the party.

Feelings

upset

angry

surprised

confused

proud

relieved

worried

scared

Family members SB p.40

1 ★★☆ **Do the crossword. Find the famous father of Maddox, Pax, Zahara, Shiloh, Knox and Vivienne in the shaded squares.**

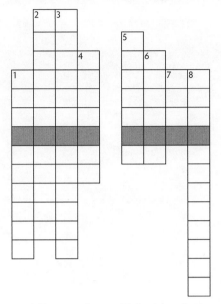

1 My parent's son. He's older than me.
2 He's married to my sister.
3 My son's daughter.
4 My dad's mum.
5 My mum's dad.
6 The son or daughter of my uncle.
7 My mum's sister.
8 My parent's daughter. She's younger than me.

2 ★★★ **Look at the example. Think of famous people or other people you know and write sentences about them.**

0 a little brother
   Prince Harry is Prince William's younger brother.

1 a big sister
   _____

2 a father-in-law
   _____

3 cousins
   _____

4 a grandpa
   _____

5 an uncle
   _____

6 a sister-in-law
   _____

7 an aunt
   _____

Feelings SB p.43

3 ★★☆ **Unscramble the words in the list. Write them under the pictures.**

~~purerissd~~ | cusdefno | droup | drewori
deliever | credas | estup | grany

0 *surprised*   1 _____

2 _____   3 _____

4 _____   5 _____

6 _____   7 _____

4 ★★☆ **How do you feel when …**

0 you watch a horror film?
   I feel scared!

1 you get bottom marks in a test?
   _____

2 you get top marks in a test?
   _____

3 you don't understand a lesson?
   _____

4 your best friend forgets your birthday?
   _____

5 you've got an important test in the morning?
   _____

6 a test is over (and it wasn't so difficult)?
   _____

7 your grandparents give you some money (and it's not even your birthday)?
   _____

READING

1 REMEMBER AND CHECK **Complete the sentences. Then check your answers in the article on page 39 of the Student's Book.**

0 Marge Simpson is Homer's _wife_ .

1 Homer is Lisa and Maggie's _____

2 Ben's on _____ with his Grandpa and Gwen.

3 Ben and Gwen, the two _____ , fight quite a lot.

4 Greg is the middle _____ of the Heffley family.

5 He is Roderick's _____ brother.

2 Read the TV guide quickly. What relationship is …

1 Joe to Lucy? _____

2 John to Paul? _____

3 Read the TV guide again. Are sentences 1–7 'Right' (A) or 'Wrong' (B)? If there isn't enough information to answer 'Right' or 'Wrong', choose 'Doesn't say' (C).

0 *We're Watching You* is on twice a week.
  A Right   **B** Wrong   **(C)** Doesn't say

1 There are famous actors in the show.
  A Right   **B** Wrong   **C** Doesn't say

2 The show makes the reviewer laugh.
  A Right   **B** Wrong   **C** Doesn't say

3 The families behave badly for the camera.
  A Right   **B** Wrong   **C** Doesn't say

4 No-one in the Collins family is happy with what they watch.
  A Right   **B** Wrong   **C** Doesn't say

5 Anna Collins is good at sport.
  A Right   **B** Wrong   **C** Doesn't say

6 The Lawson family like action films.
  A Right   **B** Wrong   **C** Doesn't say

7 Saturday nights don't usually have a happy ending for the Lawsons.
  A Right   **B** Wrong   **C** Doesn't say

4 Answer the questions.

0 Why do people like watching the show?

  It's really funny.

1 What does Joe and Lucy's dad like watching?

  _____

2 What does Joe's sister want?

  _____

3 Whose grandpa can't hear very well?

  _____

4 What does John's grandson want to do?

  _____

TV Guide: *We're Watching You*

Watching TV families watching TV

We're Watching You is a simple but brilliant idea; put a tiny camera on the front of the TVs in several family homes and record them, and then make it into a TV programme. And that's all it is, a TV programme that shows us real people watching real TV. Exciting? Not really. But it is really, really funny.

Of course, all the people on the show agree to the camera being on their TV but they soon forget it's there and then the problems start.

There are the Collins family from Huddersfield. Mike, the dad, can never find the remote control, and soon starts shouting at his kids, Joe and Lucy, to find it. Of course, as his wife Anna says, he always finds it – he usually sits on it. Anna only wants to watch sport, her husband wants cooking programmes, Joe wants cartoons and Lucy wants a quiet house without TV. No-one usually gets what they want.

And then there's the Lawson family from Taunton. They sit down together and watch a film every Saturday night. It always starts off well but soon there's action. Grandpa John can't hear very well. He always wants to turn the volume up. This upsets his daughter, Georgia, who hates the loud noise. So Grandpa turns it down, but then he asks his grandson, Paul, to tell him what people say. This makes Paul angry. And then his mum often walks in front of the TV into the kitchen to get a cup of tea. Poor Paul – he doesn't want a cup of tea, he just wants to watch the film.

We're Watching You is fun to watch but I'm glad these cameras aren't in my home!

72

DEVELOPING WRITING

An invitation

1 Read the invitations. Put the events in the order that they start on Friday.

1	The sleepover
	The film
	The school show
	The party

A

Hayden,

Can you come to my birthday party at The Fun Factory? It's on Friday evening from 6 pm to 10 pm. They do food there so don't eat before! Please let me know if you can come so I can tell the organisers how many people to expect. Hope you can come.

Best,

Don

B

Joe,

Do you want to go to the cinema on Friday to see the new Bond film? There's a show at 7 pm so we can meet at 6 pm and have a pizza at the café, if you'd like. Let me know if you can come.

Ian

C

Dear Aunt Beth,

There's a show on at my school next Friday and I'm in it. I'd love it if you could come. It starts at 6.30 pm but get there early if you want a good seat. The school's at the beginning of Brook Lane. There's a lot of space to park. Hope to see you there.

Dawn

D

Dear Jasmine,

Would you like to come to a sleepover at my house this Friday? We can come and pick you up at about 5 pm and take you back on Saturday afternoon. Please say 'yes'. We'll have fun.

Susie

PS My mum says you have to ask your parents first.

2 Look at the lines from the replies. Match them with the invitations.

0   Mum and Dad want me back before lunch if that's OK.   **D**

1   By the way, what do you want for a present?   ☐

2   I can be there at 6 pm. I want a seat right in the front row!   ☐

3   Sorry, I can't be there at that time. I'd love to see it. Is there a later show – around 8 pm?   ☐

Writing tip: An invitation

If you want someone to do something with you, you might send them an invitation.

- Invitations don't need to be long but they do need to contain all the important information – what the event is, where it is, what time it starts, etc.
- If you know the person well you might not need to include information such as where you live or your telephone number. So think carefully about what the important information is.
- If the invitation is to a friend, use more informal language and make your invitation sound friendly. Remember, you want this person to say 'yes'. Use expressions to make them feel very welcome; *please come, I hope you can come, please say 'yes'*, etc.
- More formal invitations need more formal language. Address the person with *Dear* and use expressions like *Would you like to come ... ?* rather than *Do you want to ... ?*
- Don't forget to ask for a reply.

3 Write an invitation (50–60 words). Choose one of these reasons.

1   You want your teacher to come and watch your band play on Friday evening.

2   You want your best friend to play tennis after school.

3   You want your friend to go away with you and your family for the weekend.

_____

_____

_____

_____

_____

_____

LISTENING

1 🔊**17** Listen to the conversations. Put the pictures in order.

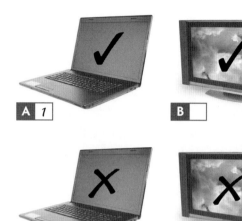

A `1`   B ☐

C ☐   D ☐

2 🔊**17** Listen again. Mark the statements T (true) or F (false).

0 In conversation 1 the girl wants to do her homework. `T`

1 The girl can borrow her mum's laptop. ☐

2 In conversation 2 the girl can't borrow her mum's laptop. ☐

3 In conversation 3 the boy wants to play a video game. ☐

4 He says his homework is for Thursday. ☐

5 In conversation 4 the father gives the boy the remote control. ☐

3 Put the words in the correct order to make conversations.

1 A I / laptop / Can / borrow / your?

0 *Can I borrow your laptop?* _____

   B Why / to / you / borrow / do / it / want?

1 _____

   A want / I / homework / to / do / my.

2 _____

   B can / course / OK, / you / of.

3 _____

2 A we / TV / Can / watch / some?

4 _____

   B homework / you / Have / any / got?

5 _____

   A Friday / it's / Yes / only / but / for.

6 _____

   B you / no / can't / Well. your / Do / first / homework.

7 _____

DIALOGUE

1 Write a conversation for each of these pictures Use a request in each conversation, with a positive answer in one, and a negative answer in the other.

TOM _____

ALAN _____

TOM _____

ALAN _____

SALLY _____

MUM _____

SALLY _____

MUM _____

▆▆▆ TRAIN TO THiNK ▆▆▆

Making inferences

1 Look at the text on page 40 of the Workbook again. Who do you think says these things? Choose from the names in the list.

John | Georgia | Paul | Mike | Joe | Anna | Lucy

0 What did he say? *John*

1 It's my turn and we're watching football. _____

2 Can't we just turn it off! _____

3 Shh! They're giving us a really good recipe for a cake. _____

4 Why don't you look under your legs? _____

5 No, Mum, I don't want anything to eat, thank you! _____

6 Where is it? I want to change channel. _____

7 Can you turn it up a bit? _____

8 Not tennis again. I want to watch *Batman*. _____

9 Please – turn it down! _____

CAMBRIDGE ENGLISH: Key

Reading and Writing part 6

1 Read the descriptions of family members. Complete the words.

0 My mum's mum g _r a n d m a_

1 My mum's dad g _ _ _ _ _ _

2 My mum's sister a _ _ _

3 My mum's brother u _ _ _ _

4 The children of 2 or 3 above

   c _ _ _ _ _ _ _

Exam guide: word completion

In the word completion activity you read five definitions and you have to write the word. You are given the first letter.

- In this activity it's important that your spelling is correct, so it's a good idea to write the words on a piece of paper before you write on the answer sheet.
- Make sure your answers have the right number of letters – there is one letter for each gap.
- Always read the instructions carefully – they tell you what category of words you have to think of (e.g. 'family members').
- Always learn words in groups, as you can find them on the third page of every unit in this Workbook. This helps you to remember words better.

2 Read the descriptions of feelings. Complete the words.

0 When you aren't happy u _p s e t_

1 When you really don't know what to do

   c _ _ _ _ _ _ _ _

2 When you don't expect something

   s _ _ _ _ _ _ _ _ _

3 When you are a bit nervous about something

   w _ _ _ _ _ _

4 When you are happy because a bad thing is over

   r _ _ _ _ _ _ _

Listening part 3

1 🔊18 Listen to Olivia talking to Dave about her family. For each question, choose the right answer A, B or C.

0 Beth's husband is …

   A French.   B Scottish.   Ⓒ Irish.

1 Olivia has got …

   A one sister.   B two sisters.   C three sisters.

2 Luke is …

   A 8 weeks old.   B 8 months old.   C 8 years old.

3 Olivia's grandpa is called …

   A William.   B Tony.   C Roger.

4 Dave thinks Olivia looks like her …

   A cousin.   B mother.   C father.

Exam guide: multiple-choice listening

In the multiple-choice listening question, you will hear a conversation between two people. You have to choose the correct option to complete sentences about the conversation.

- Before you listen, read through all the questions. This will tell you what the listening is about.
- Look at each question carefully and identify the kind of information you need to listen out for.
- The questions come in the same order that they are in the listening. This will help you not to get lost while you listen.
- Don't worry if you miss the answer to one question. Just move on to the next one.
- You'll hear the conversation twice. Use the second time to listen for missing answers and check the answers you already have.
- Finally, don't leave an answer blank. Always have a guess.

2 🔊19 Listen to Liam talking to Rachel about a new restaurant. For each question, choose the right answer A, B or C.

0 The new restaurant is …

   A French.   B Italian.   C Mexican.

1 The restaurant is in …

   A High Street.   B River Street.   C Bridge Street.

2 Rachel was there last …

   A Friday.   B Wednesday.   C weekend.

3 Her meal was …

   A £9.   B £9.50.   C £10.

4 Rachel was there …

   A with her family.   B in the afternoon.   C for her birthday.

CONSOLIDATION

LISTENING

1 ◀))20 **Listen to the conversation.** (Circle) **A, B or C.**

1 What does the man want to drink?

   A orange juice   B water with ice   C water
                    and lemon

2 What does the young woman want to drink?

   A mineral water   B tea   C lemonade

3 What soup would the man like to have?

   A mushroom   B chicken   C tomato

2 ◀))20 **Listen again. Answer the questions.**

0 Why does the man order mineral water?

   Because there isn't any orange juice.

1 What does the waitress bring the man?

2 Whose is the drink?

3 In the third conversation what does the man want to eat?

4 What does he think about the place?

5 Where does he arrange to meet Lisa?

GRAMMAR

3 (Circle) **the correct word.**

1 **A** Is that your book?

   B No, it's *her / hers*.

2 **A** Is that your grandpa's watch?

   B Yes, it's *his / hers*.

3 **A** Have you got a cat?

   B Yes, I have. *It's / Its* name is Tigger.

4 **A** Do you like your new phone?

   B Yes, I do and *it's / its* got a really good camera too.

5 **A** *Whose / Who's* are those trainers?

   B They're mine.

4 (Circle) **the correct words.**

NATALIE   *[0]Was / (Were)* you at the cinema with Joan and Lucas last night?

JOSEPH   Yes, I *[1]was / were*. It *[2]was / were* a lot of fun.

NATALIE   And then? *[3]Was / Were* you all at the fast food place again?

JOSEPH   How do you know? We *[4]was / were*, actually.

NATALIE   Oh, I also know what you had. You always have *[5]some / any* sausages, *[6]a lot of / much* chips, and you don't eat *[7]some / any* vegetables.

JOSEPH   Yeah, I know. I don't eat *[8]too much / enough* healthy food, you're right.

NATALIE   Hey, I've got an idea. Come and have lunch at our place. My dad's a good cook. He's a vegetarian so he doesn't cook *[9]some / any* meat but he makes *[10]much / lots of* excellent salads.

JOSEPH   Thanks, that sounds good.

NATALIE   Well, come tomorrow at 12.30.

JOSEPH   Great, thanks.

VOCABULARY

5 **Unscramble the adjectives in brackets. Complete the sentences.**

0 How would you like your vegetables,   *boiled* (deilob) or *grilled* (llrigde)?

1 This curry is too _____ (ypisc) for me, I'm afraid.

2 I'm sorry, but this smells so _____ (unstsdgiig) that I can't eat it.

3 **A** Do you think the soup's too _____ (aslyt)?

   B No, not at all. I think it's very _____ (yttas).

4 This steak is nice, and the salad's _____ (cidesliou).

5 **A** How do you like the _____ (staro) chicken?

   B It's absolutely _____ (uymym).

6 These vegetables are all really _____ (hefrs).

7 This cheesecake's just not very good. It's too _____ (weset), and it tastes a bit _____ (igorbn).

44

6 Complete the sentences. Use words for family members and feelings. Use the ideas in brackets and the first letters to help you.

0 It's my *little sister's* (I'm her big brother) birthday next week. She doesn't know that I'm organising a party. She'll be very *surprised* when she finds out.

1 My _____ (mother's father) loves taking photos. He's always p_____ when he can show them to us.

2 My _____ (uncle's wife) was in hospital for a few days. We're all r_____ she's OK again.

3 My _____ (uncle's daughter) Joanna hates horror films. They make her really s_____.

4 Roy and Christina are _____ and wife (married). They are u_____ because their daughter Caroline never visits them.

DIALOGUE

7 Complete the conversation. Use the phrases in the list.

~~can I borrow~~ | feel really bad | what about
didn't mean to | can I, please | a couple of
I'm so sorry | don't worry | of course | that's OK

ZOE   Jordan, 0 *can I borrow* your MP3 player?

JORDAN   1_____ you can. Your big brother never says 'no', does he?

ZOE   That's right. Thanks so much. Bye.

JORDAN   Where are you going?

ZOE   I'm going to meet Mia and Emily.

JORDAN   And 2_____ my MP3 player? Are you taking it with you?

ZOE   3_____? It's only 4_____ hours. I'll be back soon.

JORDAN   5_____. But make sure you bring it back.

(later)

JORDAN   Ah, you're back.

ZOE   Well, yes, but I 6_____. The MP3 player. It's broken.

JORDAN   I can't believe it.

ZOE   7_____, Jordan. I 8_____ break it. It was an accident.

JORDAN   OK, 9_____. These things happen. But next time … Your big brother will say 'no'!

READING

8 Read the magazine article about unusual birthday traditions. Mark the sentences T (true) or F (false).

Happy birthday – the world over

HOW do you celebrate your birthday? With a cake, a party for your friends, with games and fun for all? In some countries birthday celebrations are really unusual.

In some parts of India, for example, when a child has their first birthday, their parents cut off all their hair. The birthday child wears colourful clothes and gives chocolate to all their friends.

In Vietnam, they celebrate everybody's birthday on New Year's Eve. Parents give their children a paper envelope with coins in it – 'lucky money'.

In Korea, they celebrate day number 100 after the child is born. Children get rice cakes with honey and red and black beans. Families make sure a child gets a lot of these rice cakes. When a child gets a hundred rice cakes this means that they will live a happy and long life.

When children in Denmark wake up on their birthday, there are presents all around the bed on the floor. That's why some of the children are so excited that they find it difficult to fall asleep the night before!

0 In India children get chocolate from their friends on their birthdays. ☐ F

1 Parents in some parts of India cut off their children's hair on their first birthdays. ☐

2 In Vietnam they only celebrate children's birthdays on the last day of the year. ☐

3 In Korea they celebrate before a child is four months old. ☐

4 Children in Korea get lots of rice cakes with chocolate and ice cream. ☐

5 In Denmark children get their presents the night before their birthdays. ☐

WRITING

9 Write a paragraph about how you celebrate your birthday (about 80–100 words). Use the questions to help you.

- How important are birthdays in your family?
- How do you celebrate them?
- Are there any interesting traditions?

5 IT FEELS LIKE HOME

GRAMMAR
Past simple (regular verbs) SB p.50

1 ★☆☆ **Find nine more verbs in the word search and write them next to the past forms.**

S	T	A	Y	D	U	T	S	T	W	L
T	W	T	R	E	V	I	R	R	A	P
O	R	M	D	V	E	S	U	T	N	A
P	L	A	N	K	L	I	K	E	T	S
L	I	R	E	R	R	V	A	R	N	W

0	_stay_	stayed	5	_____	studied
1	_____	liked	6	_____	wanted
2	_____	arrived	7	_____	visited
3	_____	planned	8	_____	stopped
4	_____	dried	9	_____	used

2 ★★☆ **Use the past tenses in Exercise 1 to complete the sentences.**

0 The bus _arrived_ thirty minutes late.

1 We _____ to go to the beach.

2 The test was really important so I _____ all weekend for it.

3 I really _____ the film. It was so funny.

4 We _____ my uncle in Spain for our holidays.

5 We _____ in a really expensive hotel on our last holidays. It was great.

6 She _____ playing football because of an accident.

7 I _____ my birthday party very carefully. I wanted it to be perfect.

8 My hair was wet so I _____ it with your towel.

3 ★★☆ **Write the past forms of the verbs.**

0	call	_called_	6	love	_____
1	start	_____	7	ask	_____
2	try	_____	8	finish	_____
3	seem	_____	9	look	_____
4	watch	_____	10	show	_____
5	enjoy	_____	11	decide	_____

4 ★★★ **Complete the story with the past forms of the verbs in brackets.**

When I was younger I ⁰ _loved_ (love) LEGO. My sister and I ¹_____ (play) with it all the time. I always ²_____ (ask) for LEGO for my birthday. I was a member of the LEGO Club. Every three months a magazine ³_____ (arrive) in the post. It was full of ideas for models you could build and there were photos of models from club members. Each time I ⁴_____ (open) the magazine, I ⁵_____ (look) at that page for hours. I ⁶_____ (dream) of seeing one of my models on that page. One day my sister and I ⁷_____ (decide) to build the best model ever and send a photo to the magazine. For days we ⁸_____ (work) on it. We ⁹_____ (use) so many different types of bricks, big ones, small ones, square ones, round ones, red ones, blues one – every shape and colour you can imagine. After about a week we ¹⁰_____ (finish). It was amazing and we were so happy. Then we ¹¹_____ (need) to take a photo of it. Very carefully I ¹²_____ (pick) it up and ¹³_____ (carry) it down the stairs. My sister ¹⁴_____ (open) the kitchen door and there were three more steps to the kitchen table. Unfortunately, the dog was sitting between me and the table. He ¹⁵_____ (jump) up and ¹⁶_____ (knock) the model to the floor. It ¹⁷_____ (smash) into thousands of pieces. We ¹⁸_____ (try) to fix it but it was useless. I ¹⁹_____ (look) at my sister and we both ²⁰_____ (realise) it was the end of our dream.

Pronunciation
Regular past tense endings
Go to page 119.

Modifiers: *quite, very, really* `SB p.51`

5 ★★☆ **Write sentences with the words in brackets.**

0 I'm not happy today. (very)
I'm not very happy today.

1 Your grandmother is young. (really)
_____

2 Hurry up. We're late. (very)
_____

3 Can I have a sandwich? I'm hungry. (quite)
_____

4 I'm tired. I want to go to bed. (quite)
_____

6 ★★☆ **Circle the best word.**

0 It's 40°C today. It's *quite /* (*really*) hot!
1 That song's OK. It's *quite / very* good.
2 This bed is so uncomfortable. It's *quite / very* hard.
3 The sea's *quite / very* cold today. Don't go in it. You'll freeze!
4 That food is *quite / really* delicious. I want to eat it all.

Past simple negative `SB p.53`

7 ★☆☆ **Match the sentence halves.**

0 I chatted to her for an hour ___ *c*
1 He downloaded the game ___
2 She posted the card on Monday ___
3 He cooked them a really special meal ___
4 The team played really well ___

a but it didn't arrive for my birthday.
b but we didn't win.
c but we didn't talk about you.
d but they didn't really like it.
e but it didn't work.

8 ★★☆ **Make the sentences negative.**

0 I liked the ice cream.
I didn't like the ice cream.

1 We enjoyed the film.
_____

2 They went to France for their holidays.
_____

3 She wanted to go to the party.
_____

4 He won 1st prize in the photography competition.
_____

5 You met Dan at my party.
_____

9 ★★☆ **Complete Jenny's holiday blog with the correct form of the words in the list.**

not like | not look | ~~arrive~~ | not think
stop | not work | not want | want

Day 8 Ice cream in Rome

We ⁰ _**arrived**_ in Rome last night at about 7 pm. Dad really wanted to see the Trevi fountain. I ¹_____ to see it. I wanted to watch some TV and get an early night. But Dad is the boss and so we all followed him there. Then Dad asked me to take a photo of him by the fountain. He ²_____ very cool in his silly hat so I refused. He ³_____ that very much. On our way back to the hotel we ⁴_____ to buy some ice cream. I didn't want to stop. I just ⁵_____ to get to bed. But Dad, as I already said, is the boss so we stopped. Well, this time I was wrong. What a fantastic ice cream. It was delicious. The best ice cream ever. I ⁶_____ an ice cream could taste so good! Anyway, we arrived back in the hotel about 10 pm. I tried to watch some TV but it ⁷_____ so I just went to bed and dreamed about ice cream all night.

GET IT RIGHT!
Past simple (regular verbs)

We add -ed to verbs ending in vowel + -y (e.g. *played*).
✓ *play – played*
✗ *play – plaid*

If the verb ends in consonant + -y (e.g. *try*), we change the -y to -i and add -ed.
✓ *try – tried*
✗ *try – tryed*

Correct the past simple forms.

1 plaid   _____
2 staid   _____
3 studyed   _____
4 tryed   _____
5 enjoied   _____
6 tidyed   _____

VOCABULARY

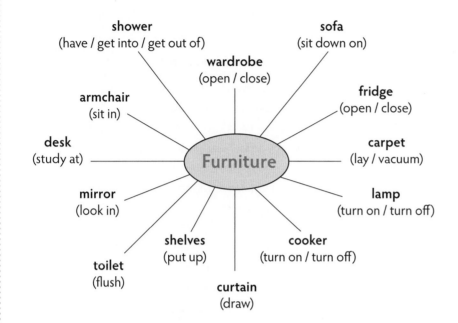

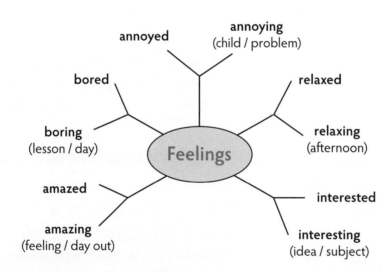

Look

look up
(a word / a person)

look into
(a crime)

look at
(a picture)

look after
(children / pets)

look for
(your keys)

Key words in context

charity	My dad gives money to a **charity** that helps children in poor countries.
creative	She's a writer so she always has very **creative** ideas.
care for	This charity **cares for** dogs that have no home.
work together	Let's **work together** and finish this job quickly.
uncomfortable	This sofa is **uncomfortable**. We need a new one.
comfortable	My bed is really **comfortable**. I don't want to get out of it in the mornings.
untidy	Your room is **untidy**. There are books and clothes all over the floor.
safe	You're **safe** now. There's no danger anymore.
at home	I don't think Bob is **at home**. All the lights are off.
homeless	There are many **homeless** people living on the streets in London.
pay attention	I want you to stop talking and **pay attention** to me.

Furniture SB p.50

1 ★★☆ **Use the sentences to complete the crossword.**

ACROSS

3 Ian is looking at his hair in the ___.
5 Liam is standing at the ___ in the kitchen making dinner.
8 Tim is putting his clothes in the ___.
10 Don't turn the ___ off. I'm using it to read.
11 Priscilla is washing her hair in the ___.
12 Ollie is doing his homework at his ___.

DOWN

1 The dog is lying on the floor on the ___ in front of the TV.
2 Mum is sitting in the ___ reading the newspaper.
4 Bob is sitting with Sally and Jim on the ___.
6 Ben's little brother over the road is watching us from behind the ___.
7 Dad is putting his books up on the ___.
9 Can I use the ___ before we go out? Yes, it's in the bathroom upstairs.

2 ★★★ **What are your favourite pieces of furniture? Choose three pieces and write about each one.**

I love the armchair in our living room because it's very comfortable.

1 _____
2 _____
3 _____

-ed and -ing adjectives SB p.53

3 ★☆☆ **Find nine more adjectives in the word snake and write them below.**

0 *bored*
1 _____
2 _____
3 _____
4 _____
5 _____
6 _____
7 _____
8 _____
9 _____

4 ★★☆ (Circle) **the correct adjective.**

0 This sunset is (amazing) / amazed.
1 This lesson is *boring / bored*.
2 I love holidays. They're so *relaxed / relaxing*.
3 We broke Mr Evans's window with our ball. I think he is a bit *annoying / annoyed* with us.
4 I passed the exam! I'm *amazing / amazed*.
5 Don't turn the TV off, Dad. This programme is really *interesting / interested*.

WordWise SB p.55

Phrasal verbs with *look*

5 ★☆☆ **Match the questions with the replies.**

0 What are you looking at? — `d`
1 What does 'circulation' mean? — ☐
2 Did you find out what happened to your sandwich? — ☐
3 Do you want to come to my house after school? — ☐
4 What are you looking for? — ☐

a I don't know. Let's look it up in the dictionary.
b I can't. I've got to look after my little brother.
c My pen. I can't find it anywhere.
d Some old photos.
e No – it's a mystery but I'm still looking into it.

6 ★★☆ (Circle) **the correct option to complete the sentences.**

0 The police are looking (into) / after / up / for what happened last night.
1 I looked *after / up / for / at* her number in the phone book.
2 Look *up / for / at / into* that bird. It's amazing.
3 My mum and dad are looking *for / to / into / after* a new house.
4 She helps her dad look *at / into / after / up* her little brothers.

READING

1 | REMEMBER AND CHECK | **Read the article on page 49 of the Student's Book again. What do the numbers refer to?**

0 Half past four _____time_____

1 1,200 _____

2 More than 3 million _____

3 Seven weeks _____

4 17 _____

5 22 _____

2 Read the article quickly, then write the name of the country under the photos.

1 _____

2 _____

3 _____

Some of us live in big houses, some of us live in small houses. Some of us live in apartments in very tall buildings, some of us live in bungalows next to the sea. But most of us live in houses that look like … well … houses. But not everyone. Some people like things that are a bit different and that includes their home. For example, there's a house that looks like a strawberry in Japan, another one that looks like a mushroom in Ohio, USA, and there's a toilet-shaped house in South Korea. There's even a house in Poland that is completely upside down!

Maybe you know the children's poem about the old lady who lived in a shoe. In Pennsylvania, USA there is a real shoe house. Of course, it's not really a shoe, just a house in the shape of a shoe. A local shoe manufacturer called Mahlon N. Haines had the idea of building it. He used it as a guesthouse. When he died it became an ice cream shop for a while. These days, it's a museum.

The One Log House in Garberville, California, USA is a one-bedroom house inside the trunk of a 2,000-year-old giant redwood tree. It took two people seven months to remove all the inside of the tree and make a living space that is just over two metres high and nearly 10 metres long.

Joanne Ussary from Benoit, Mississippi in the USA lives in a plane. It's a Boeing 727, without the wings. The plane cost $2,000 and it cost another $4,000 to move it on to her land. She spent another $24,000 making it into a home.

It's not the only 'flying' home in the USA. In Chattanooga there is a house in the shape of a spaceship; a round white disc with four legs.

And believe it or not, there is a walking house in Denmark. It's a hexagonal tube supported by six metal legs. It can move over most surfaces. It is a collaboration between Danish artists and scientists. Moving home couldn't be any easier. When you want to live somewhere new, just push a button and walk your house to a new location.

3 Read the article again. Answer the questions.

0 What is the shoe house in Pennsylvania today? _____It's a museum._____

1 How old is the tree trunk of the One Log House? _____

2 How much did Joanne Ussary spend on turning the plane into a home? _____

3 Who built the walking house in Denmark? _____

4 Which two houses have legs and how many legs have they got? _____

5 How many houses in the article are in the USA? _____

DEVELOPING WRITING

A blog

1 Read the blog entry. Tick (✓) the things that Mia writes about.

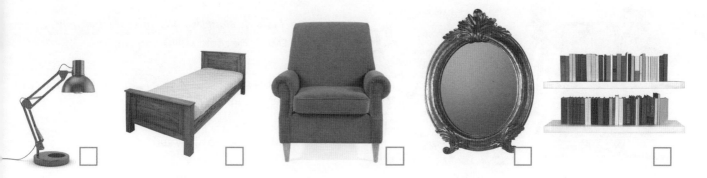

POSTED: TUESDAY 5 JANUARY

Welcome to my world – my room

Next to the bathroom at the top of the stairs in my house is a very special room. It's a small but cosy room. It's a special room because it's the place where I feel most at home in the whole world. It's my bedroom.

I love my bedroom. It's bright and friendly. The walls are light blue and it's got a big window. The sun shines through it every morning. There's a comfortable blue bed, a small wooden desk and some shelves where I keep all my favourite books. On the walls there are some really cool posters of my favourite films.

I always feel really relaxed in my bedroom. It's the only room in the house where I can be on my own, away from all the noise of my family. I always go there to do my homework, read a book, listen to music or just to lie on the bed and think. I never feel bored in my bedroom.

Labels: my room, special place   **16 comments**

2 Complete the sentences from the text with the missing adjectives.

0 It's a ___*small*___ but ___*cosy*___ room.

1 I love my bedroom. It's _____ and
   _____ .

2 There's a _____ _____ bed

3 A _____ _____ desk.

Writing tip: adjectives

● We can use more than one adjective to make our writing more descriptive.

● If the adjectives come after the noun or pronoun we use *and* or *but* to separate them. Look at example sentences 0 and 1. Why do we use *but* in sentence 0 and *and* in sentence 1?

● If the adjectives come before the noun we don't use *and*, however, we need to be careful about the order we use them. The usual order is: my opinion / size / colour / what it's made of.

● Try not to use more than two adjectives.

3 Look at the three paragraphs of Mia's blog. Which paragraph …

a describes the room?

b talks about how the room makes Mia feel?

c introduces the room and says where it is?

4 Think about your favourite room.

1 Where is it?

   _____

2 Describe it. What's it got inside?

   _____

3 How do you feel when you are there? Why?

   _____

4 Think of some good adjectives to use.

   _____

5 Write a blog about your favourite room in about 100–130 words. Use Mia's blog and the language above to help you.

LISTENING

1 🔊**23** Listen to Dan and Emily talking about raising money. Tick (✓) the things they talk about.

TOYS

BOOKS

2 🔊**23** Listen again and complete the sentences with no more than four words.

0 They want to raise money for people who lost ___*their homes*___ in an earthquake in China.

1 Danny wants to raise _____ of money.

2 Most of Emily's toys _____ or have bits missing.

3 Danny thinks that most people use _____ to clean their cars.

4 Tickets for the rock festival will cost _____ .

5 They can use the _____ for the rock festival.

6 They need to get permission _____ for the festival.

DIALOGUE

1 Put the words and phrases in order to make parts of the dialogue.

0 **DANNY** to raise / something / money / let's do / a lot of

   Let's do something to raise a lot of money.

1 **EMILY** we could / think / do you ?

   _____

2 **DANNY** and sell / we get / old toys / why don't / all our / them?

   _____

3 **EMILY** not / so / I'm / sure.

   _____

4 **EMILY** their cars / going round / how about / and washing / for them / to people's houses ?

   _____

5 **DANNY** think / good idea / that's a / I don't

   _____

PHRASES FOR FLUENCY `SB p.55`

1 Put the dialogue in order.

- [ ] **A** Oh no! But I know what you mean – he gets angry really easily.
- [1] **A** Did Chris invite you to his party?
- [ ] **A** Well, I hope you come anyway.
- [ ] **A** What did you say?
- [ ] **A** Hang on. Why not? I thought you were friends.
- [ ] **B** We were. But I said something he didn't like and now he doesn't talk to me.
- [ ] **B** No he didn't. It's no big deal, though.
- [ ] **B** To be honest, I don't want to.
- [ ] **B** I just said he wasn't a very good footballer. He got really angry with me.
- [ ] **B** Anyway, it's not my problem he's angry. And I really don't care about his silly party.

2 Complete the sentences. Use words in the list.

~~deal~~ | honest | problem | hang | mean | though

1 **A** Why are you so annoyed? It's really not a big ___*deal*___ .

   B Maybe it isn't. I'm still angry, _____ .

2 **A** I don't want to go to the match, to be _____ . I don't really like football.

   B I know what you _____ . It is really boring.

3 **A** _____ on. We can't just leave this dog here on the street.

   B Of course we can. It's not our _____ .

CAMBRIDGE ENGLISH: Key

Reading and Writing part 5

1 **Read the article about home. Choose the best word (A, B or C) for each space.**

What is a home?

For ^{0}_____ home is a place where I feel safe at all times. It is a place where I always feel welcome. It is always full of friends ^{1}_____ family. Home is more than just a house. It's the street where I live too. It's the park ^{2}_____ the bottom of the road. It's the shops where I ^{3}_____ my comic every week and where I get my crisps and sweets. When I walk down ^{4}_____ streets, I see the friendly faces of people who know my name and say 'hello'. I stop to talk to these people to find out what is ^{5}_____ in their lives. They ^{6}_____ me questions about my life too.

   When someone stops and asks me for directions I know where he ^{7}_____ to go and I can tell him the best way to get there. Home is a place where I ^{8}_____ ask other people for directions.

Example:

0	A mine	B my	C me		
1	A and	B so	C but		
2	A in	B at	C over		
3	A bought	B buy	C buys		
4	A that	B this	C these		
5	A happen	B happened	C happening		
6	A ask	B say	C tell		
7	A want	B wanted	C wants		
8	A always	B sometimes	C never		

Exam guide: multiple-choice cloze

In a multiple-choice cloze, you are given three choices of words that could fit the gap to complete a text. You must select the correct one.

- Read all the text to understand what it is about.
- Look at each gap carefully. Look at the words before and after it. Can you guess what word is missing without looking at the answers? If your guess is one of the options, then it is probably the correct answer.

- If you can't guess the word, look at the answers. Put each one in the gap and read the sentence to yourself in your head. Which one sounds correct?
- If you are not sure which is the correct word, then cross out the ones that don't sound right and choose one of the others.
- Always choose an answer even if you have no idea which one is correct.

2 **Read the story. Choose the best word (A, B or C) for each space.**

Last week my mum and dad decided to get a cleaner to come and clean the house ^{0}_____ a week. They both work and they don't have ^{1}_____ time to do the housework. They arranged for the cleaner to come ^{2}_____ Monday morning. I was very surprised when my dad asked ^{3}_____ to tidy my room on the Sunday. 'What about the cleaner?' I asked. 'We have to tidy a bit,' he said. 'The house ^{4}_____ a mess.' So I tidied my room, Mum tidied the rest of the house and Dad vacuumed. Then Dad started cleaning the windows and Mum started cleaning the fridge and the cooker and the rest of the ^{5}_____ . They cleaned from morning to evening and when they finished the house ^{6}_____ sparkling clean. The next morning the cleaner came. I went ^{7}_____ school and Mum and Dad went to work. When we got home later in the afternoon there ^{8}_____ a note on the kitchen table. It was from the cleaner. 'I'm sorry,' it read, 'I can't clean your house. There is nothing to clean!'

Example:

0	A one	B first	C once		
1	A much	B many	C lots		
2	A in	B at	C on		
3	A I	B me	C my		
4	A is	B was	C be		
5	A bedroom	B bathroom	C kitchen		
6	A were	B is	C was		
7	A for	B in	C to		
8	A is	B was	C were		

6 BEST FRIENDS

GRAMMAR
Past simple (irregular verbs) SB p.58

1 ★★★ Write the past simple forms of these verbs. Use the irregular verb list on page 128.

0	know	_knew_	6	drink	_____
1	buy	_____	7	have	_____
2	bring	_____	8	say	_____
3	take	_____	9	tell	_____
4	eat	_____	10	get	_____
5	leave	_____	11	cost	_____

2 ★★☆ Complete the crossword.

ACROSS

1 Yesterday we _____ a really good film.

4 His name is Bill? Really? I _____ it was Brian.

8 We met last year. We _____ really good friends.

9 It was my sister's birthday. I _____ her a CD.

10 Last night I _____ my homework.

DOWN

1 My dad played the guitar and I _____ a song.

2 I _____ to the cinema three times last week.

3 I liked the blue shirt and the red one. In the end I _____ the red one.

5 We had a party last night. We _____ a lot of noise!

6 We _____ a strange noise, but it was only the wind.

7 When he came in to the room, everyone _____ up.

8 The match _____ at three o'clock.

3 ★★★ Complete the text with the verbs in brackets in the past simple form. (Careful! Some verbs are regular and some are irregular).

It was hard to believe, but it was true – a concert by Kings of Leon, in our town! When I [0] _saw_ (see) the poster, I [1]_____ (phone) all my friends to tell them. At first they [2]_____ (not believe) me, but then they all [3]_____ (get) really excited!

We all really [4]_____ (want) to go to the concert – it was our favourite band and we [5]_____ (hear) that you could buy tickets online. The tickets were too expensive, I [6]_____ (not have) enough money, but my dad [7]_____ (give) me some money as an early birthday present and we [8]_____ (buy) four tickets near the stage.

We were all very excited. For two weeks we [9]_____ (not talk) about anything else – just the concert. And then finally, the big day [10]_____ (arrive). My friends [11]_____ (come) to my house and we all [12]_____ (get) ready. Then we [13]_____ (take) a bus to go to the concert.

We [14]_____ (have) a great time at the concert. The band [15]_____ (play) really well and they [16]_____ (perform) for three hours! My friends and I [17]_____ (sing) too, because we [18]_____ (know) the words to every song! Unfortunately they [19]_____ (not sing) my favourite song, but you can't have everything, I guess.

After the show we all [20]_____ (go) to a fast food place. We [21]_____ (eat) hamburgers and [22]_____ (talk) about the show. Allie [23]_____ (say) it was the best concert ever – and we [24]_____ (think) the same!

Double genitive SB p.59

4 ★★☆ For each sentence, circle the correct answer (A, B or C).

0 Last week I met a friend of ... .
   A you   B your   **C yours** ⃝

1 He gave me a jacket of ... .
   A him   B his   C he

2 Oh, yes, Jack and Sue are very good friends of ... .
   A ours   B our   C us

3 I don't know her, but she's a cousin of ... .
   A Johns'   B John's   C John

4 I love their music. I've got eight CDs of ... .
   A them   B their   C theirs

5 I found out that our teacher is an old friend of ... .
   A my father's   B me father   C my father

Past simple: questions SB p.61

5 ★★☆ Use the words in brackets to form questions. Then use the information in brackets to write the answers.

0 _Did you like_ the film yesterday? (you / like)
   Yes, I did. (✓)

1 _____ any clothes at the weekend?
   (he / buy)
   _____ (✗)

2 _____ a lot of photos last weekend?
   (you / take)
   _____ (✗)

3 _____ with you to the party? (your friends /
   go)
   _____ (✓)

4 Who _____ in town this morning? (you / see)
   _____ (Jenny)

5 Where _____ on holiday last year?
   (they / go)
   _____ (Corfu)

6 What _____ for dinner last night? (you / eat)
   _____ (pizza)

6 ★★★ Complete the questions.

0 I saw someone yesterday.
   Who _did you see_ ?

1 I bought something last week.
   What _____ ?

2 They went somewhere last weekend.
   Where _____ ?

3 I heard something.
   What _____ ?

4 You said something.
   What _____ ?

5 She told me something.
   What _____ ?

6 I met someone.
   Who _____ ?

7 I found the answer somewhere.
   Where _____ ?

8 I phoned her last night.
   Who _____ ?

GET IT RIGHT! 👁

Past simple: questions

We form past simple questions with question word + *did* + subject + base form of the verb. Remember to use *did* in the correct place.

✓ Where **did** you **meet** your friend?
✗ Where ~~you met~~ your friend?
✗ Where ~~you did meet~~ your friend?

Write a cross (✗) next to the incorrect sentences. Then write the correct sentences.

1 Why you didn't come to my party? ☐
   _____

2 What you did at the weekend? ☐
   _____

3 Where did they go on holiday? ☐
   _____

4 Who you went to the cinema with? ☐
   _____

5 What he saw at the cinema? ☐
   _____

VOCABULARY

Past time expressions

last: last night, last week, last year

yesterday: yesterday morning, yesterday afternoon

ago: five years ago, an hour ago, two weeks ago

Personality adjectives: cheerful, confident, boring, easy-going, jealous, funny, intelligent, generous, horrible, helpful

Irregular past participles

buy	bought
come	came
choose	chose
find	found
give	gave
get	got
have	had
leave	left
make	made
say	said
see	saw
stand	stood
think	thought
take	took
go	went

Possessive pronouns

I	mine
you	yours
he	his
she	hers
it	its
we	ours
they	theirs

Key words in context

certainly	I love parties, so I will **certainly** come to yours!
friendship	It was the start of a great **friendship**.
go surfing	It's a great day to **go surfing** – look at the sea!
have an accident	Be careful when you cross the street – I don't want you to **have an accident**.
in public	It's OK to do that at home, but not **in public**!
myth	A lot of people think it's true, but it isn't – it's just a **myth**.
patient	I know you're hungry, but be **patient** – dinner will be ready in 15 minutes.
right now	No, I can't wait – I want it **right now**!
save someone's life	Firemen often **save people's lives**.
score	The final **score** was 3–1.
stressed	It's an important exam, so I'm a bit **stressed** right now.
upset	It was very bad news, so she was **upset**.

Past time expressions SB p.58

1 ★☆☆ (Circle) the correct option.

0 I saw her two weeks (ago)/ yesterday.

1 Where were you *last / yesterday* afternoon?

2 He arrived *last / yesterday* week.

3 We started school five years *ago / last*.

4 I tried to phone you three hours *ago / afternoon*.

5 I didn't feel well *last / yesterday* morning.

6 We went out *last / yesterday* night.

2 ★★☆ Complete the puzzle. What is the 'mystery word'?

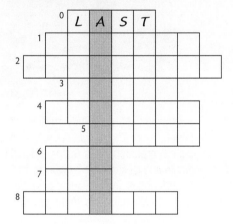

0 We went to the cinema ____last____ Sunday.

1 The time now is 7.25. _____ minutes ago, it was 7.10.

2 Today is Monday. _____ was Sunday.

3 It's 25th August. Two _____ ago it was the 11th.

4 I was late for school this _____ .

5 I watched a great film last _____ .

6 I was born fifteen years _____ .

7 It's December. _____ months ago it was October.

8 We went out to a restaurant yesterday _____ .

3 ★★★ Complete each sentence about you / your family / your country, or anything / anyone else you know.

0 Two years ago, *my sister got married* .

1 Last night, _____ .

2 Three weeks ago, _____ .

3 _____ an hour ago.

4 Fifty years ago, _____ .

5 Last Sunday, _____ .

6 _____ yesterday morning.

7 Last year, _____ .

8 Yesterday afternoon _____ .

Character adjectives SB p.61

4 ★★☆ Complete the adjectives and then match them with the definitions a–i.

0 *f u n n y* ☐ f

1 _ _ _ p f _ _ ☐

2 _ _ t _ _ l _ _ _ _ t ☐

3 _ h _ _ _ f _ _ ☐

4 _ _ _ _ y- _ _ _ n _ ☐

5 g _ _ _ _ _ _ u _ ☐

6 _ _ _ _ f _ d _ _ _ _ ☐

7 _ _ a l _ _ _ s ☐

8 b _ _ i _ _ ☐

a relaxed and not easily worried

b happy and positive

c unhappy because you want something someone else has

d happy to give other people money, presents or time

e not interesting or exciting

f making you smile or laugh

g certain about your ability to do things well

h happy to help others

i able to learn and understand things easily

5 ★★☆ Look at these character adjectives. Which ones do you think are positive (P), or negative (N)?

☐ cheerful   ☐ confident

☐ easy-going   ☐ funny

☐ horrible   ☐ generous

☐ helpful   ☐ jealous

☐ intelligent   ☐ boring

6 ★★☆ Choose four adjectives from Exercise 5. Write sentences about yourself.

I'm usually a cheerful person.

I'm not really jealous at all.

_____

_____

_____

_____

Pronunciation

Stressed syllables in words

Go to page 119. 🔊

READING

1 REMEMBER AND CHECK For each sentence, (circle) the correct option. Then check your answers in the article on page 57 of the Student's Book.

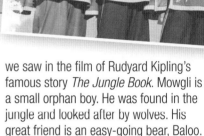

0 *Charlotte* / (*The music teacher*) suggested that the two friends could sing together.

1 Jonathan wasn't sure about going on TV because of his *appearance* / *voice*.

2 When they came onto the stage they were very *relaxed* / *nervous*.

3 One judge on the TV show said that *Jonathan* / *Charlotte* should sing alone.

4 They *won* / *came second* in the TV competition.

5 Their first CD was called *Two of Us* / *Together*.

2 How many of the friends in the photos can you name? Read the text quickly and check your ideas.

Famous friends in literature

As we all know, having friends is really important in our lives. But of course there are also great friendships in books and films – and some of them are very famous.

In JK Rowling's books, Harry Potter's two great friends are Hermione and Ron. Harry relies on them a lot and they often help him in difficult situations. And though they don't always all agree on everything, they're friends for life.

Back in the nineteenth century, an American writer called Mark Twain created two characters called Tom Sawyer and Huckleberry Finn. They lived in southern USA near the Mississippi River. Together they had problems with their families and with slavery.

Also in the nineteenth century, in Britain, Sir Arthur Conan Doyle created one of the most famous detectives ever: Sherlock Holmes. His friend, Dr Watson became very famous too … and Watson always tried to help Holmes. In a recent film, the two friends were played by Robert Downey Junior and Jude Law.

Meanwhile in 1844, over in France, Alexandre Dumas wrote *The Three Musketeers*. The characters Athos, Aramis and Porthos were in a special part of the King's Army and fought against injustice. Together with D'Artagnan, they showed their friendship with a cry of: 'All for one, and one for all!' These famous friends have also appeared in films on many occasions over the years.

OK, so what about a friendship between a boy and a bear? That's what we saw in the film of Rudyard Kipling's famous story *The Jungle Book*. Mowgli is a small orphan boy. He was found in the jungle and looked after by wolves. His great friend is an easy-going bear, Baloo. He helps Mowgli in his fight against the dangerous tiger, Shere Khan.

There are many stories about friendships between men or boys (and there's Baloo too), but famous stories about friends don't seem to include many girls or women. There's *Little Women*, of course – Louisa May Alcott's story of four sisters in New England and how they love each other, but they were sisters and not just friends. Has anyone out there got some great female literary friendships, please?

3 Read the text again. Answer the questions.

1 Who are Harry Potter's friends?

_____

2 When did Mark Twain write his stories about two friends?

_____

3 Which friends shouted: 'All for one, and one for all'?

_____

4 What did Baloo help Mowgli to do?

_____

5 Why is *Little Women* different from other examples of friends?

_____

4 Do you know any other famous friendships in stories or in films, or on TV? Write two sentences.

I read a book where there are three friends called …

_____

_____

I saw a film …

_____

_____

_____

DEVELOPING WRITING

An apology

1 Read the messages. Match them with the answers. There is one extra answer!

> *Hello Thomas,*
>
> *I'm sorry I didn't come to your birthday party. My aunt and uncle came to visit us on Saturday, and Kylie and James, my cousins, were with them. We always get on very well with each other. To be honest we were all together and when I remembered about your party it was too late. I didn't want to phone you, so I'm writing to explain what happened. I hope you can forgive me! I'm really sorry.*
>
> *Jeremy*
>
> **B**

> Hi Clare,
>
> I'm writing to say I'm so sorry about what happened last week. I don't know why we started to fight. I'm really sorry for the things I said. I hope we can still be friends because I really like you. Oh, I've got tickets for the concert on Sunday. Would you like to come with me? Please say yes.
>
> John
>
> **C**

> Dear Joanne,
>
> Sorry about what I said yesterday about people who use mobile phones all the time. I really didn't know that your grandma was ill. I understand you wanted to phone her, and I'm really sorry that I hurt you. I hope you're not angry with me any more. I made a mistake, but I really didn't want to hurt you.
>
> Love,
> Karen
>
> **A**

☐ 1 Hi … , Thanks for telling me. I didn't understand why you didn't come to the party. Now I do and I'm not angry because we all make mistakes. Next time – don't forget!

☐ 2 Hi … , How could I be angry? Your message is so funny! It's OK you forgot about the money. Let's not talk about it any more. I can't wait to see your present.

☐ 3 Hi … , Thanks for writing. Do you know what? I kind of feel the same. There wasn't really a reason to start a fight. And, yes, we are normally great friends. Thanks for the invitation, but I can't come. It's my dad's birthday this weekend.

☐ 4 Hi … , Thanks so much for writing. I'm really not happy myself when people have their mobiles on all the time. Only it was different for me this time. Thanks for understanding! I hope we can meet soon.

Writing tip: informal messages

When you send an email or another message to a friend, use an informal style of writing.

- Begin your message with *Hi* (name), or *Hello* (name). You can use *Dear* (name) in informal and formal messages.
- Use short forms, e.g. *I'm*, *We didn't*, *you aren't*, etc.
- Make it personal. For example, use sentences such as: *I'm sorry about what happened. I hope we can still be friends. You know I really like you. Please say yes.*
- End your message with one of the following: *Love,* (name); *Cheers,* (name); *Take care,* (name); *Hope to hear from you soon,* (name); or use only your name.

2 Write an email to apologise. Choose one of the following situations.

LISTENING

1 🔊26 Samantha is telling Jack about a man and his cat. Listen and find out their names.

2 🔊26 Listen again. (Circle) the correct answers.

1 At first, Jack …
  A thinks the story of the cat is very interesting.
  B thinks Samantha's telling him a joke.
  C isn't interested in the story.

2 James became a writer. His book is about …
  A the time when he played music for little money.
  B how his friendship with a cat changed his life.
  C people in London and their pets.

3 Bob the Cat …
  A is now well known and may become a film star.
  B can do some tricks and play the guitar.
  C is now living in a home for street animals.

4 Jack would like to …
  A have a cat like Bob.
  B watch the film about Bob.
  C read the book too.

3 🔊26 Listen again. Complete each space with between one and three words.

1 James was a street musician, sitting on _____ and playing his guitar.

2 When James saw the cat for the first time, it had a problem with _____ .

3 When James went home on the underground, the cat _____ him.

4 When James had the cat near him, more people stopped and gave him _____ money.

5 James decided to write a book about his _____ the cat.

6 Samantha thinks that about _____ people bought *A Street Cat named Bob.*

DIALOGUE

1 🔊27 Listen to the sentences. Write the past tense verb you hear in the spaces. Then put the sentences in the correct order.

| 1 | A | What ___*did*___ you do in London at the weekend? |

☐ B Indian food? I'm sure you _____ Indian. I know it's your favourite.

☐ C And what _____ that?

☐ D Yes, it's delicious, isn't it? And I'm sure you _____ lots of things as well.

☐ E Well, yes, I _____ some nice clothes in the shops but I only _____ one thing.

☐ F Oh, we _____ lots of things. And we _____ some great food.

☐ G Of course! But we _____ some Chinese food, too. That _____ nice.

☐ H I _____ this belt. It's for you. I'm sorry I _____ your birthday last week!

▌TRAIN TO THiNK ▌

Making decisions

1 You can invite a famous person to your birthday party. Who do you want? Write the names of three people you like in the circles.

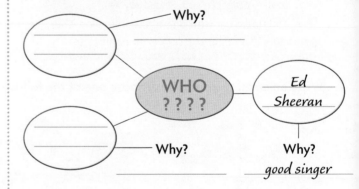

2 Next to each person write one reason for inviting him/her.

3 Use your mind map to make a decision.

4 Write a sentence saying who you want and why.
I want Ed Sheeran because he can sing for me.

CAMBRIDGE ENGLISH: Key

Listening part 2

1 🔊**28** Listen to Kevin telling Abigail about his birthday. What present did each person give him? For questions 1–5, write a letter A–H next to each person.

People		Presents	
0	Brother [C]	A	book
1	Sister [ ]	B	sports shoes
2	Mum [ ]	C	DVD
3	Dad [ ]	D	tickets
4	Aunt [ ]	E	camera
5	Granddad [ ]	F	video game
		G	laptop
		H	money

Exam guide: matching

In Listening part 2 you are given a list of five items, and a list of eight different items. You must listen to a dialogue and match each of the five items with an item from the other list.

- Before listening, quickly read through the two lists.
- Listen carefully – the first object you hear is not always the correct answer. In the example above, you hear:

    Abigail: *What did you get from your sister?*

    Kevin: *Well, she usually gives me a book, but this time she bought me this video game. It's a sports game. It's great fun to play.*

- Sometimes, you will not hear exactly the object you see in the list, but a 'paraphrase' – a word or group of words that mean the same as another word. In the example below from Exercise 1 when Kevin says *trainers* he is talking about *sports shoes*. Example:

    Abigail: *Oh! And what did your mum give you? Some money?*

    Kevin: *No, she bought me these <u>trainers</u>? Do you like them?*

2 🔊**29** Listen to Charlotte talking to her friend Christian about a photo of her old school friends. What clothes were her friends wearing? For questions 1–5, write a letter A–H next to each person.

People		Their clothes	
0	Ella [G]	A	jacket
1	Jacob [ ]	B	trousers
2	Olivia [ ]	C	belt
3	Cynthia [ ]	D	jumper
4	Sylvia [ ]	E	shorts
5	Adam [ ]	F	trainers
		G	dress
		H	shirt

Reading and Writing part 2

1 Read the sentences about a TV talent show. Choose the best word (A, B or C) for each space.

1 Last year I _____ to enter a talent show.

   A decided   B realised   C thought

2 I sang a song in front of three _____ .

   A audience   B contestants   C judges

Exam guide: multiple-choice sentences

In Reading and Writing part 2 you have to complete a sentence from a choice of three words. The sentences are all about the same topic or tell a simple story. This exercise tests vocabulary, not grammar.

- Read the sentence without looking at the words. Try to guess what the missing word is.
- Check the words. Is the word you guessed one of them? If it is, then that is probably the correct answer.
- If the word you guessed isn't one of the options, read the sentence in your head and put each of the words in turn into the gap. Which word sounds best?

2 Read the sentences about friends. Choose the best word (A, B or C) for each space.

0 Steve and Allan are _____ friends.

   (A) best   B first   C better

1 They _____ at school when they were five years old.

   A made   B met   C knew

2 They get _____ really well.

   A on   B over   C together

3 They're really _____ friends and they share all their secrets.

   A near   B far   C close

4 They never fight or _____ arguments.

   A do   B make   C have

5 They have a great _____ .

   A friends   B friendly   C friendship

CONSOLIDATION

LISTENING

1 🔊30 **Listen and tick (✓) the correct room.**

A ☐

B ☐

C ☐

2 🔊30 **Listen again and answer the questions.**

1 Why does she like blue walls?
2 Why does she like the fact that her desk is near the window?
3 When did she get her new wardrobe?
4 Who gave her the money for the wardrobe?
5 How did they know that she didn't like her old wardrobe?
6 How does her sister feel about the new wardrobe?

GRAMMAR

3 **Complete the conversation. Put the verbs in brackets into the correct form of the past simple.**

JASON I ⁰ ___went___ (go) to a party at Jack's house on Friday. It was great.

PAUL Good. I'm happy that you ¹_____ (like) it. Jack's parties are good fun.

JASON Yes, they are. I ²_____ (dance) with Alison Gardner. We ³_____ (have) a great time there!

PAUL Yes, Alison's nice. I ⁴_____ (take) her to the cinema three weeks ago. We ⁵_____ (see) a great film.

JASON That's nice. But you ⁶_____ (not go) to Jack's party! Why not?

PAUL Jack ⁷_____ (not invite) me. He ⁸_____ (have) another party two months ago, and he ⁹_____ (invite) me to that.

JASON Two months ago? I ¹⁰_____ (not know) that! Now I'm annoyed!

PAUL Oh. I ¹¹_____ (say) the wrong thing. Sorry.

VOCABULARY

4 **Complete each adjective. The first letter is already there.**

0 She always understands what's happening. She's very i _n_ _t_ _e_ _l_ _l_ _i_ _g_ _e_ _n_ _t_ .

1 I'm sure I passed the exam. I'm very c _ _ _ _ _ _ _ _ _ about it.

2 The film was awful! I was really b _ _ _ _ _ .

3 I love the new mirror in your room! I'm really j _ _ _ _ _ _ _ !

4 After a long day, I like to have a long, r _ _ _ _ _ _ _ _ shower!

5 I was late with my homework again. The teacher was quite a _ _ _ _ _ _ _ with me.

6 He looks sad today. He usually smiles and looks c _ _ _ _ _ _ _ _ .

7 The game yesterday was great – really a _ _ _ _ _ _ _ ! I loved it.

8 She was very h _ _ _ _ _ _ and painted my room with me.

5 (Circle) **the correct options.**

Near our town there's a famous old house where some rich people lived about two hundred years ⁰*last* / (*ago*). Last weekend my mum said, '¹*Why* / *How* about going to visit that house?' And we did. I brought a friend of ²*my* / *mine* with us. We ³*went* / *go* by bus and my mum ⁴*paid* / *took* for us all to go in. I didn't really want to go at first because I'm usually ⁵*boring* / *bored* by museums and things. But when we got there, I thought it was ⁶*amazing* / *amazed*.

The house has got about sixty rooms and they were really ⁷*interesting* / *intelligent*. There was an enormous ⁸*sofa* / *desk* – I'm sure twenty people could sit on it! The windows were really big with beautiful red ⁹*carpets* / *curtains* on them. My dad ¹⁰*took* / *take* a photograph in one of the rooms, but a man working there got ¹¹*annoyed* / *annoying* because there was a sign that said: 'No photographs!'

DIALOGUE

6 Complete the conversation. Use the words in the list.

~~bored~~ | about | ago | boring | could | didn't | enjoy | let's | sure | thought | went | why

MIKE   I'm so ⁰ ___*bored*___

JANINE   How ¹_____ going for a walk?

MIKE   No, I ²_____ for a walk yesterday. ³_____ do something here in the house.

JANINE   A computer game! ⁴_____ don't we play a computer game?

MIKE   No. Do you remember? We played on the computer last Saturday and I ⁵_____ win a single game!

JANINE   Oh yes, I remember! I ⁶_____ it was great fun.

MIKE   Yes. But I didn't ⁷_____ it very much.

JANINE   Sorry, Mike. It's just a joke, OK? But here's an idea. We ⁸_____ watch my new DVD. I bought it two days ⁹_____ .

MIKE   I'm not so ¹⁰_____ . Is it one of those romantic films? They're so ¹¹_____ .

JANINE   No, don't worry. It's an adventure. Come on, let's try it.

READING

7 Read this newspaper article about making decisions. (Circle) the correct ending (A or B) for each sentence.

1 Psychologists at a university in the USA wanted to find out
   A if teenagers and their friends are good car drivers.
   B what decisions teenagers make when they are with friends.

2 They noticed that teenagers behaved in a more dangerous way when
   A they thought their friends were not watching.
   B they thought their friends were watching them.

3 The experiments show that teenagers need to be careful about making decisions when
   A they are with their friends.
   B they are on their own.

WRITING

8 Write a paragraph about you and your decisions in about 80 words. Use the questions to help you.

- How often do you make decisions? What type of decisions are easy / difficult?
- Do you ever ask for advice when making a decision?
- With your friends do you make decisions for the group or does someone else?

_____

_____

_____

_____

_____

_____

_____

When teens make BAD DECISIONS

PSYCHOLOGISTS at Temple University in Philadelphia, USA did an interesting experiment. They asked teenagers to play a video game that involved car driving. They could win prizes for driving fast. But the faster they drove, the bigger their risk was of losing the prize money. Half the time, the teenagers played the game on their own, and half of the time the psychologists told them that their friends were in the room next door, watching them. The results were fascinating: when the teens played the game on their own, they made much better decisions. When they thought their friends were watching, their driving was much more dangerous. They drove faster, had more accidents, and often didn't stop at red lights.

Psychologists say that teens should think carefully before making important decisions when their friends are present!

7 | THE EASY LIFE

GRAMMAR

have to / don't have to `SB p.68`

1 ★☆☆ **Match the sentences with the signs.**

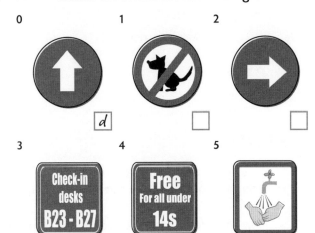

0   1   2

d   ☐   ☐

3   4   5

Check-in desks B23 - B27   **Free For all under 14s**

☐   ☐   ☐

a You don't have to go to terminal A for flights to Paris.

b You have to wash your hands.

c Drivers have to turn right here.

d You have to go straight ahead.

e You have to leave your dog outside.

f Children don't have to pay.

2 ★★☆ **Write the sentences.**

0 the / a lot / have / we / Maths / study / test / to / for
We have to study a lot for the Maths test.

1 be / to / to / creative/ have / find / answer / We / the

_____

2 Sundays / make / to / has / he / On / breakfast

_____

3 early / you / get / have / Do / to / up / ?

_____

4 Lucas / school / tomorrow / have / doesn't / to / to / go

_____

5 have / I / phone / Do / to / you / ?

_____

6 me / to / You / have / help / don't

_____

3 ★★☆ **Match the questions and answers.**

0 Does your dad have to travel a lot in his job?   `d`

1 Can I come to your place tomorrow?   ☐

2 Why can't Susan come with us to the beach?   ☐

3 Does your brother live in the city centre?   ☐

4 Can I go to the match on Sunday?   ☐

5 Why can't I go to the cinema tonight?   ☐

a I spoke to her dad. She has to help at home.

b No, he doesn't. He has to take a train every day.

c I'm afraid you can't. We have to visit Grandma.

d Yes. He goes to other countries quite a lot.

e Because you have to tidy up your room.

f I'm sorry. You have to study for school. But why don't you go tomorrow?

4 ★★★ **Answer the questions so they are true for you.**

1 Do you have to get up early on weekdays?

_____

2 Do you have to use the Internet for your school work?

_____

3 Does your best friend have to help at home a lot?

_____

4 Do you have to do homework over the weekend?

_____

should / shouldn't `SB p.69`

5 ★☆☆ **Circle the correct words.**

0 The film starts in 10 minutes. We're late, so we *should* / *shouldn't* hurry up.

1 Dad doesn't know when he'll be home and says we *should* / *shouldn't* wait for him to eat.

2 It's just a T-shirt. Why does it cost £65? It *should* / *shouldn't* be so expensive.

3 Why are you angry with me? You *should* / *shouldn't* try to understand me.

4 She's on holiday until Monday. We *should* / *shouldn't* phone her before then.

5 Jane doesn't like her school uniform. She thinks students *should* / *shouldn't* wear what they want.

6 ★★☆ Complete the conversations. Use *should* or *shouldn't* and a phrase from the list.

~~put on a jumper~~ | stay much longer | talk to her
worry so much | leave home earlier

0 A I'm feeling cold.
   B I think you *should put on a jumper* .

1 A I can't believe it. I'm late for school again!
   B Perhaps you _____ .

2 A I don't think Jane is very happy at all.
   B Maybe you _____ .

3 A I'm a bit nervous about my English test.
   B You _____ . It's not helpful.

4 A It's getting late.
   B Yes, I know. We _____ .

7 ★★★ Answer the questions. Your answers can be funny or serious. Give reasons.

0 Should children get money for helping at home?
   Yes, they should because parents get money
   for their work too.

1 Should students get money for going to school?

2 Should the Internet be free for everybody?

3 Should every child have a tablet?

mustn't / don't have to   SB p.70

8 ★☆☆ Look at the rules for a youth hostel. (Circle) the correct words in the sentences.

HOSTEL HOUSE RULES
- Last time for check out: 11.30 am.
- Music? OK, but use headphones.
- Switch off lights at 10 pm!
- Breakfast 7.30 – 9.30 am.
- Please wash up after eating.
- Don't walk into the bedrooms with your shoes on.

0 You (mustn't) / don't have to have the lights on after 10 pm.
1 You mustn't / don't have to leave the dinner table without cleaning up.
2 You mustn't / don't have to play music out loud.
3 You mustn't / don't have to wear your shoes in the bedrooms.
4 You mustn't / don't have to check out before 10 o'clock.
5 You mustn't / don't have to have breakfast at 7.30.

9 ★★☆ Match the sentences and complete them with *mustn't* or *don't have to*.

0 My parents aren't very strict.   `e`
1 Sarah hasn't got any problems with her work. ☐
2 The test will be hard.   ☐
3 It's a secret.   ☐
4 The doctor says Ella's fine.   ☐
5 Thanks for Jim's number.   ☐

a You _____ help her.
b I _____ forget to call him.
c You _____ tell anyone.
d She _____ take medicine any longer.
e I *don't have to* do anything in the house.
f You _____ forget to study every day now.

10 ★★★ Answer the questions so they are true for you.

1 What work do you have to do at home?

2 What are two things you mustn't do in your class?

3 Name three things you have to do during the week, but not on a Sunday.

4 What does your friend have to do that you don't have to do?

GET IT RIGHT! 👁

Have (got) to / don't have to / must / mustn't / should / shouldn't

We always use the base form of the verb after *have (got) to / don't have to / must / mustn't / should / shouldn't*.

✓ You **should ask** your sister to help you.
✗ You should ~~to ask~~ your sister to help you.

(Circle) the correct verb form.

1 You don't have to *making / made / make* coffee. We've got a coffee machine.
2 That music is very loud. You should *use / to use / using* headphones.
3 You must *be / to be / being* careful. It's dark in the garden.
4 He shouldn't *worry / worried / worrying* about the exam. He always gets good marks.
5 Tell Sarah she mustn't *forget / to forget / forgot* to tidy her room.
6 What do I have to *doing / do / did* to join this club?

VOCABULARY

Expressions with *like*

like (Ryan)
(it) looks like …
(it) sounds like …
Like what?

Key words in context

dream come true	Going on safari in Africa would be a **dream come true**!
illness	After a long **illness** she returned to work.
invention	The wheel was a fantastic **invention**. It changed our lives.
care about someone/something	I really **care about John.** I want to do something to help him.
environment	I think we should all protect the **environment** better.
appearance	Do you care a lot about your **appearance**?
quality	How important for you is the **quality** of your work?
inventor	Thomas Edison was a famous **inventor**.
have access to something	Do you think students should **have access to the Internet** during exams?
switch off	Let's **switch off** the computer now. It's time to relax!
robot	I'd love a **robot** that did all the housework.
create problems	You're giving him his own computer! Are you trying to **create problems**?
fair	Mum says I can't have a phone until I'm 11. It's not **fair**!

Gadgets SB p.68

1 ★☆☆ **Do the crossword. Can you find the mystery word?**

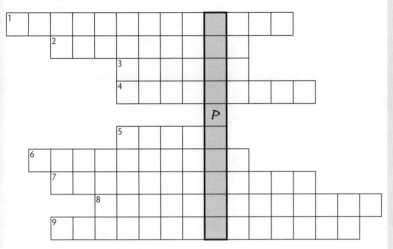

1 Many people need it to make a drink for their breakfast.
2 An electronic gadget that allows you to store music in a special format and play it.
3 Drivers use it to find their way.
4 You need it when your hair is wet.
5 A small light you hold in your hand; it usually has a battery.
6 A small electronic device that helps you with numbers.
7 The controls for a machine to play games.
8 A gadget that allows you to switch an electronic machine on or off from a distance.
9 A piece of electrical equipment to which another piece of equipment can be connected.

Housework SB p.71

2 ★☆☆ **Match the sentences and their endings.**

0 Luke's friends are staying for lunch. Can [f]
1 There are no clean plates left. Can you
2 I dropped some sugar on the floor. Will you
3 My room is a mess, but I'm too lazy
4 Can you do the cooking tonight? I did it
5 I'll do the washing, but I really don't want
6 We have no food left in the house. Can you
7 Can you load the dishwasher, Sarah?
8 My mum showed me how to make my bed

a do the washing up quickly?
b yesterday, and the day before yesterday.
c to tidy it.
d when I was still a child.
e do the shopping if I tell you what we need?
f you set the table, please?
g But it's Pete's turn. I emptied it this morning.
h help me vacuum it?
i to do the ironing too.

3 ★★★ **What housework do you like/dislike? Write four sentences about you.**

I don't like ironing clothes. I think it's boring.
I don't mind doing the cooking. It's cool when the others like my food.
I hate … . I think it's … .

WordWise SB p.73

Expressions with *like*

4 ★☆☆ **Match the sentences and the pictures.**

0 Jane's like her mum. They both love nature. [c]
1 It looks like a heart.
2 I think Dad's home. That sounds like his car!
3 It smells like an apple, but it doesn't look like one.

READING

1 **REMEMBER AND CHECK** (Circle) the correct option, A–C. Then check your answers in the text on page 67 of the Student's Book.

0 How did Ludwick Marishane get the idea for his invention?

    A A friend gave it to him.   **(B)** from talking with friends.   **C** He got it from the Internet.

1 What's a big problem for 2.5 billion people?

    A They've got trachoma.   **B** Their water is dirty.   **C** Medication is too expensive for them.

2 When Ludwick was at university, he spoke to a lot of people about …

    A money.   **B** his ideas.   **C** the name of his invention.

3 From the first idea to the production of 'DryBath', it took more than …

    A three years.   **B** ten years.   **C** two years.

4 Ludwick is very much interested in …

    A making money.   **B** not having to take a bath.   **C** helping people.

2 Read the article quickly. Write the name of the inventions under the photos.

1 _____

Change for the better

When Emily Cummins was four years old, her grandfather gave her a hammer. She loved using it, and started to learn how to make toys from old things that nobody used any more.

When she was a teenager, she thought a lot about making inventions to help other people. Emily's other granddad had an illness called arthritis. He had a lot of pain in his hands and fingers. One day, Emily saw that he had problems getting toothpaste out of the tube. She made an invention that helped him with this, and won the Young Engineer for Britain Award for her toothpaste dispenser.

A few years later, Emily learnt about the situation in some African countries where women and children often walk many kilometres a day to get water for their villages. They can only carry one bucket a time, and they usually put them on their heads. Emily's invention is a simple water carrier. It's made of wood, so it's easy to repair. For example, the 'wheel' on the water carrier is made from branches of trees. It makes it possible for the women to transport up to five buckets each time. They don't have to carry it on their heads.

2 _____

Her latest project is a simple fridge that runs without electricity using only the energy that comes from the sun. There are now thousands of families in villages in Zambia, Namibia and South Africa who use it to keep milk, food and medicines cool.

Emily is now a young woman. She is the winner of several prizes for her inventions. She was named one of the world's top ten young people. She also got the Peace Honours Prize from a jury of Nobel prize winners during an awards ceremony in Norway.

Emily frequently visits schools and talks to teenagers. She wants to inspire them to come up with new ideas that make the world a better place. She wants to use her skills to make a difference. She isn't interested in making a bigger TV or better sound system. She wants to create change for the better.

3 Read the article again. Are sentences 1–5 'Right' (A) or 'Wrong' (B)? If there isn't enough information
✳ to answer 'Right' or 'Wrong', choose 'Doesn't say' (C).

0 As a child, Emily loved making things herself.   **A** Right   **B** Wrong   **C** Doesn't say

1 At the age of 13, she invented a toothpaste dispenser.   **A** Right   **B** Wrong   **C** Doesn't say

2 When she went to Africa, she got an idea for a water carrier.   **A** Right   **B** Wrong   **C** Doesn't say

3 Her latest project is a solar ice cream machine.   **A** Right   **B** Wrong   **C** Doesn't say

4 Emily got a prize in Norway.   **A** Right   **B** Wrong   **C** Doesn't say

5 She'd like to invent a high quality sound system.   **A** Right   **B** Wrong   **C** Doesn't say

DEVELOPING WRITING

Taking notes and writing a short summary

1 Read the text. Tick (✓) the things that Alexander Graham Bell experimented with.

A famous inventor

When Alexander Graham Bell was 29, he made one of the most important inventions in the history of the world: the telephone. A year later, he started the Bell telephone company. It became very successful. He became a businessman and earned a lot of money from his telephone company.

But Alexander Graham Bell wasn't so interested in money. He was interested in making inventions. He always wanted to learn, and to try and create new things. He never stopped thinking of new ideas. He used his money to open laboratories with teams of engineers who could help him make his dreams come true.

Bell was also fascinated with propellers and kites, and did lots of experiments with them. In 1907, four years after the Wright Brothers made their first flight, Bell formed the Aerial Experiment Association with four young engineers. Their plan was to build planes. The group was successful. Their plane named Silver Dart made the first successful flight in Canada on 23 February, 1909.

2 Look at a student's notes on the first paragraph of the text in Exercise 1. <u>Underline</u> the ideas in the text that the student used.

1 *29 invented telephone*
2 *Bell telephone company*
3 *success (businessman)*
4 *lot of money*

3 Write a short text using full, connected sentences. Use the notes from Exercise 2.

4 Read the second and third paragraphs of the text about Alexander Bell again. <u>Underline</u> five important points and write them in the form of notes. Then write a short summary of the text based on your notes.

Writing tip: taking notes after reading a text

Read the whole text carefully.

- Go through the text again. Select the most important information. Underline it in the text and use it to write your notes.
- Write words, not sentences. Use abbreviations, e.g. *inv* for invented, *tel. co* for telephone company.
- Don't write down words that are unnecessary, e.g. *the, a, and*, etc.
- Make sure your notes are clear and meaningful. Check them again and ask yourself: Do these notes give me a good summary of the most important information in the text?
- Write up your notes.

LISTENING

1 🔊 31 Listen to the conversations. (Circle) A, B or C.

1 What's the problem?
   A The camera doesn't work.
   B The USB cable isn't plugged in.
   C The laptop doesn't work.

2 What does Daniel have to do?
   A tidy his room
   B walk the dog
   C wash up

3 What did James borrow without asking?
   A a digital camera
   B an MP3 player
   C a laptop

2 🔊 31 Listen again. Complete the sentences from the conversations.

STELLA Let [0]m *e*_____ [1]s_____. You
        [2]h_____ [3]t_____ switch
        [4]y_____ [5]c_____ on.

DANIEL Alright. [6]G_____ you. Do I
        [7]h_____ to [8]t_____ up my
        desk [9]t_____?

LILY   Well, you [10]m_____ use
        [11]m_____ [12]th_____ without
        [13]a_____.

DIALOGUE

1 Complete the conversation with the expressions in the list.

do you mean | Like what | Sorry

OLIVER I want to do a mini-triathlon on Sunday.

MAYA   [1]_____?

OLIVER A mini-triathlon. That's three races in one.

MAYA   Three races in one? What
        [2]_____?

OLIVER Well, you have to run 3 km, swim 1 km, and cycle 10 km.

MAYA   Really? That sounds like hard work. Why is it called mini?

OLIVER Because the races in a normal triathlon are much longer.

MAYA   [3]_____?

OLIVER Well, in the Olympic triathlon they cycle 40 km, run 10 km, and swim 1.5 km.

MAYA   Wow! I think we should try the mini race!

OLIVER I think you're right.

2 Write a short conversation for this picture. Use some of the expressions from Listening Exercise 2 and Dialogue Exercise 1.

PHRASES FOR FLUENCY SB p.73

1 Complete the conversation with the expressions in the list.

so | no chance | and stuff | never mind
absolutely | such good fun

MAX   [0]___*So*___, Isaac, what are you doing after school?

ISAAC After school? Why?

MAX   I just want to know if you want to play football.

ISAAC Football! [1]_____, I've got to do housework [2]_____.

MAX   OK, [3]_____. What about tomorrow? Can we play then?

ISAAC [4]_____.

MAX   Great. It's going to be [5]_____!

Pronunciation

Vowel sounds: /ʊ/ and /uː/

Go to page 120.

Reading and Writing part 1

1 Match the notices A–H with the meanings 1–5.

A **Teachers only**

B **Under 12s half price**

C **Please DON'T feed the monkeys.**

D **Wanted – waiter** ... Please enquire inside.

E **DANGER look out for trains**

F **SALE 50% off everything**

G **SWIMMING POOL** closed from 19th Oct - 12th Nov

H **Keep off the grass**

0	Be careful when you cross here.	E
1	Children pay less than adults.	
2	You mustn't give food to the animals.	
3	If you are interested in the job, come in and ask for more details.	
4	School children can't come in here.	
5	Things in this shop are half price.	

2 Match the notices A–H with the meanings 1–5.

A **Chocolate £2 each or 3 for £5**

B Baby rabbits – free to good homes

C **Last meals at 9 pm**

D **All food is homemade**

E **LOST** Black and white dog. Answers to the name of Spot.

F **PLEASE DON'T PHONE BEFORE 12 PM**

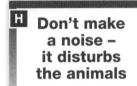

G **Magic Car Race** get yours here on Saturday morning.

H **Don't make a noise – it disturbs the animals**

0	We're looking for our pet.	E
1	You should only call them in the afternoons.	
2	You can buy the new game this weekend.	
3	It's cheaper to buy more than one.	
4	Please be quiet here.	
5	If you want to eat here, order before nine.	

Exam guide: match notices with meanings

In this exam task you have to read some notices and then match them to sentences that describe what each notice says.

- Read through all the notices. Tick the ones that you think you understand best. Look at these ones first. Try to think how you would describe what they say. Then look through the answers to see if any of them match what you think.

- If you're not 100% sure what a notice means then focus on some of the words in it that you do understand. Try to match or connect these with words in the sentences. For example, teachers and school children are obviously connected so there's a good chance these two belong together.

- Be careful – there are always more notices than sentences.

8 SPORTING MOMENTS

GRAMMAR
Past continuous SB p.76

1 ★☆☆ **Complete the text with *was* or *were*.**

It was a cold winter's morning. It ⁰___was___ raining a little. Mums and dads ¹_____ standing by the school football field. They ²_____ chatting and drinking coffee to keep warm. They ³_____ waiting for the game to begin. On the field, their daughters ⁴_____ getting ready for the big match. Some of them ⁵_____ running and others ⁶_____ kicking balls about. The goalkeeper ⁷_____ practising catching the ball. Everyone was excited. It was the final of the under 16s girls football tournament. Mr Fletcher, the headmaster, ⁸_____ cleaning his glasses. He put them on, took the whistle out of his pocket, and blew it.

2 ★★☆ **Complete the text. Choose the correct words and write them in the correct form.**

jump | take | cry | clap | sit | hold
not feel | talk | not enjoy

I got there very late. The game was over. The girls of Blacon High School ⁰___*were jumping*___ up and down. They were the champions. Their proud parents ¹_____ . One girl ²_____ up the trophy and showing it to the crowd. She wasn't being very careful and I was afraid she might drop the trophy, but luckily she didn't. A journalist ³_____ lots of photos. But not everyone was happy. The girls on the losing team ⁴_____ on the ground. Some of them had their heads in their hands and they ⁵_____ . They certainly ⁶_____ the celebrations. Mr Fletcher ⁷_____ to them but they ⁸_____ great. Another year and still no trophy.

Pronunciation

Strong and weak forms of *was* and *were*
Go to page 120. 🔊

3 ★★★ **Complete the sentences. Use the past continuous of the verbs and the information in brackets.**

0 Paula *wasn't watching TV*, she *was playing games*.
   (– watch TV / + playing games)

1 I _____, I _____.
   (– write an email / + write my blog)

2 They _____, they
   _____.
   (– speak Polish / + speak Russian)

3 We _____, we _____.
   (– fight / + play)

4 Dad _____, he _____.
   (– read / + listen to the radio)

4 ★☆☆ **Match the questions and answers.**

0 Were you listening to me? [d]
1 Was he laughing? [ ]
2 Was it raining? [ ]
3 Were they talking? [ ]
4 Was I sleeping? [ ]
5 Were we making a lot of noise? [ ]

a Yes, it was. We got really wet.
b Yes they were but I didn't hear what they said.
c Yes, I think you were.
d Yes, I heard everything you said.
e No, I don't think we were.
f No, he wasn't. He didn't think it was very funny.

5 ★★☆ **Answer the questions so they are true for you.**

What were you doing …

1 at 7 am today?
   _____

2 at 6 pm yesterday?
   _____

3 this time yesterday?
   _____

4 at 10 o'clock last Sunday morning?
   _____

Past continuous vs. past simple SB p.79

6 ★☆☆ Match the sentence halves.

0   While the teacher was talking,   **e**

1   Evan was drinking coffee   ☐

2   The boys were fighting   ☐

3   They were looking at the map   ☐

4   While I was reading in the bath,   ☐

5   I was brushing my teeth   ☐

a   and he burned his mouth.

b   when their mum walked into the room.

c   I dropped my book in the water.

d   but my toothbrush broke.

e   I put my hand up to ask a question.

f   when they realised they were lost.

7 ★★☆ Circle the correct words.

0   Matthew *played* / *was playing* the guitar when he *fell* / *was falling* off the stage.

1   I *did* / *was doing* my homework when my sister *came* / *was coming* into the room.

2   John and his sister *walked* / *were walking* to school when the accident *happened* / *was happening*.

3   I *talked* / *was talking* about Kiki when she *phoned* / *was phoning* me.

4   While Anna *tidied* / *was tidying* up her room, she *found* / *was finding* her watch.

5   While Alison *studied* / *was studying*, she *remembered* / *was remembering* it was her mum's birthday.

6   When we *found* / *were finding* out about the accident, *we watched* / *were watching* TV.

when and *while* SB p.79

8 ★★☆ Complete the sentences with *when* or *while*.

0   ___*While*___ I was trying to get to sleep, the dog started barking.

1   She was eating an apple _____ she bit her tongue.

2   We were driving in the car _____ we saw Robin on his bike.

3   _____ I was paying for the T-shirt, I realised I didn't have any money.

4   Olivia was having dinner _____ the phone rang.

5   _____ I was walking into town, I saw I had different socks on.

9 ★★★ Write two sentences about each picture.

0   Paul / jog / trip over / stone
   While Paul was jogging, he tripped over a stone.
   Paul was jogging when he tripped over a stone.

1   Gordon / rock-climb / drop / bag

   _____

2   May / windsurfing / fall / sea

   _____

3   Sue / volleyball / run into / net

   _____

GET IT RIGHT!

Past continuous

We form the past continuous with *was/were* + the *-ing* form of the verb. We use *was* with singular subjects and *were* with plural subjects.

✓ We **were playing** football when it started to rain.

✗ We ~~was~~ playing football when it started to rain.

✓ I **was windsurfing** when the accident happened.

✗ I ~~were~~ windsurfing when the accident happened.

Complete the sentences with *was* or *were*.

1   The rain started while they _____ having a picnic.

2   My friends and I _____ enjoying the competition, when the TV stopped working.

3   My brother _____ winning the race when he fell off his bike.

4   _____ you driving when it started to snow?

VOCABULARY

Word list

Sports

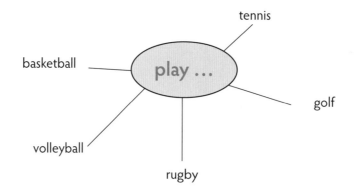

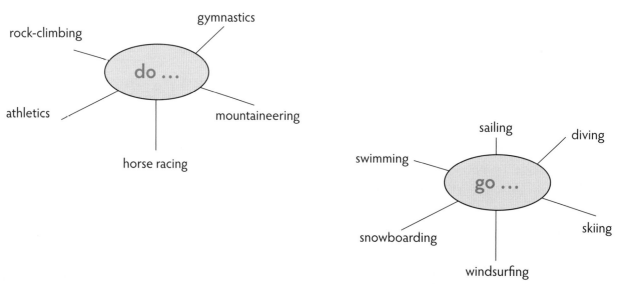

Sequencing

at first ➜ then ➜ after ➜ finally

Key words in context

marathon	The **marathon** is just over 42 km.
spectator	More than 100,000 **spectators** watched the final.
athlete	There are **athletes** from all over the world at the Olympics.
medal (bronze, silver, gold)	We didn't win a **medal** but we had a lot of fun.
stadium	The **stadium** was completely full. There wasn't an empty seat anywhere.
trophy	The captain put the **trophy** above his head and showed it to the spectators.
goal	I scored the winning **goal** in the last minute of the match.
winner	The **winner** of each race gets a gold medal.
accident	The driver had a serious **accident** but luckily no-one was hurt.
shine	The sun **is shining**. Let's go to the beach.
dream	My **dream** is to play football for Manchester United one day.
practise	You need to **practise** every day if you want to be the best.
competitive	My dad's so **competitive**. He always wants to win.
lose control	The driver **lost control** of the car and crashed into a wall.
take place	The 2014 World Cup **took place** in Brazil.
cross	The first person to **cross** the line is the winner.
grab	She **grabbed** the dog to stop it from running away.

Sports SB p.76

1 ★★☆ Use the picture clues to find the sports, then fit the sports into the word lines. The black boxes contain the last letter of one word and the first letter of the next word. There are four sports that don't fit in the word lines. What are they?

1 _____ 2 _____ 3 _____ 4 _____

| | | | | | S | | | | | | | | | | | | | | |

| | | | G | | | | | | | | S | | | | | | | | |

| | | | S | | | | G | | F | | | | | | | | | |

2 ★★★ Which sport is the odd one out in each list, and why?

0 tennis / rugby / windsurfing / basketball
Answer: _windsurfing_, because
the other sports all use balls.

1 skiing / snowboarding / swimming / ski jumping
Answer: _____, because

_____.

2 windsurfing / rock-climbing / sailing / diving
Answer: _____, because

_____.

3 tennis / rugby / volleyball / football
Answer: _____, because

_____.

3 ★★☆ Write sentences. Use the expressions in the list to start each sentence.

~~At first~~ | Finally | Then | After half an hour

0 nervous
   At first, I was nervous.

1 instructor / show / what to do

_____

2 could stand up

_____

3 ski / down the hill

_____

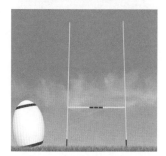

4 ★★★ Write a mini-story. Use the expressions and your own ideas.

The Tennis Game
1 At first …   3 After …
2 Then …   4 Finally …

READING

1 [REMEMBER AND CHECK] **Answer the questions. Then check your answers in the article on page 75 of the Student's Book.**

0 How long was the race Derek Redmond was running in? _400 metres_

1 How far did he run before his accident? _____

2 How many people were there in the athletics stadium? _____

3 How high is the mountain K2? _____

4 How far from the top did Gerlinde Kaltenbrunner get in the summer of 2010? _____

5 How many times did she climb K2 before she was successful? _____

1 _____

2 _____

3 _____

2 **Read the article. Match the high jumping styles with the names in *italics*.**

People who changed sport: Dick Fosbury

Like many American teenagers, Dick Fosbury wanted to be a professional sportsman but he had a problem – he wasn't very good at any sport. He didn't play football very well and although he was very tall he wasn't a very good basketball player either. He decided to try athletics. He tried running, throwing and jumping, and of all these events, he found that he wasn't too bad at the high jump.

At that time there were two popular styles of jumping over the bar. There was *the scissors*, where the athlete jumped over using his legs like a pair of scissors, and there was *the straddle*, where the athlete jumped over face first. Fosbury used the straddle. The best height he could jump was 1.63 m. It wasn't bad but it was a long way from the world record of 2.23 m.

One afternoon Fosbury decided to do something completely different.

Instead of jumping face first, he turned around and jumped back first. The results were amazing. In a few hours he improved his personal best by 21 cm. Over the next months he spent all his time practising, getting better and better. He still wasn't winning any competitions and most people were confused by his strange style. A year before the 1968 Olympics he was the number 61 jumper in the

world, and he only just made it into the USA Olympic team.

When he arrived in Mexico no one knew his name. On the day of the high jump final he walked on to the field with all the other jumpers. As the competition started, the 80,000 people in the crowd began to notice that one of the jumpers had a very strange style. At first they thought it was funny and laughed each time Fosbury jumped over the bar. After nearly four hours there were only three jumpers left. The crowd weren't laughing at Fosbury any more – they were cheering him on. The bar was at 2.24 m – a new world record. The other two jumpers knocked it off but Fosbury flew over. The gold medal was his.

Dick Fosbury was now famous all over the world and his *Fosbury flop* changed forever the way that high jumpers jumped.

3 **Read the article again. Answer the questions.**

0 Why did Fosbury choose to do the high jump? _Because it was the only sport that he wasn't bad at._

1 How high could he jump after a few hours practising his new style? _____

2 What did people first think about his new style? _____

3 How good was he at the high jump in 1967? _____

4 Was he the favourite to win the gold medal in the Olympics? Explain your answer. _____

5 How do people remember Dick Fosbury today? _____

DEVELOPING WRITING

An article

1 **Read the text below. Where do you think it comes from?**

a   A newspaper ☐

b   A school magazine ☐

c   A holiday magazine ☐

d   A story book ☐

2 **Read the text again. Where do these missing phrases go?**

0   and when we arrived, we weren't disappointed ☐A☐

1   I was soon climbing up and down the rocks. ☐

2   and we had to stop ☐

3   No-one really wanted to get onto the coach. ☐

4   and of the spectacular ocean on the other ☐

3 **Write an article for a school magazine (about 120–150 words). Choose one of these topics.**

● A sports match between your school and another one

● A school trip

● A special event that happened at the school

Fun and adventure in North Wales

Last week, year 12 students spent four nights at the Mini-Don adventure centre in North Wales. There was a lot of excitement on the coach journey there ☐A☐. The centre is in a small wood. It has views of the magnificent Welsh mountains on one side ☐B☐. We put our bags in the bedrooms, had some lunch, and then we met our friendly instructors.

Over the four days we had the chance to try out some really exciting new sports. In the mornings I chose rock-climbing. At first I was quite scared, but my instructor, Dave, was really good at keeping me calm. ☐C☐ In the afternoons I did windsurfing. It was quite difficult. On the last day I was starting to get quite good when unfortunately the weather got bad ☐D☐. Now I really want to take lessons here so I can get really good at it.

It was a shame to say goodbye to the centre on Friday morning. ☐E☐ We had a wonderful time and if you ever get the chance to go there – take it!

LISTENING

1 🔊36 Listen to the street interviews. Who does, or wants to do, these sports, the girl (G) or the boy (B)?

0 — G · 1 · 2

3 · 4 · 5

6 · 7 · 8

2 🔊36 Listen again. Mark the sentences T (true) or F (false).

0 The girl thinks the sports centre looks good. **T**
1 The girl isn't very interested in sport.
2 You can do water sports at the sports centre.
3 The boy thinks the building cost too much.
4 The sports centre has a golf course.

DIALOGUE

1 Put the words in order to make questions and answers.

0 about / sports / do / think / What / centre / you / the / new
   What do you think about the new
   sports centre?

1 brilliant / think / I / it's
   _____

2 sports / do / feel / you / centre / How / the / about / new
   _____

3 money / of / I / a / waste / it's / think
   _____

---

2 Put the sentences in order to complete the conversation.

DAN Well, we need a new swimming pool. ☐
DAN I don't agree. ☐
DAN What do you think about the new library? **1**
DAN I think it's a waste of money. There are better things to spend our money on. ☐
ANA For example? ☐
ANA I like it. I think it's really good for our town. ☐
ANA So what do you feel about it then? ☐
ANA I'm sorry but I think a library is more important than a swimming pool. ☐

▰▰ TRAIN TO THiNK ▰▰

Sequencing

1 Look at the words 1–4 in table A and the groups A–E in table B.

a What group does each word belong to?
b What position [1], [2], [3] or [4] does each word take in the group?

Table A

	Group	Position
0 afternoon	C	2
1 baby		
2 today		
3 Saturday		
4 wake up		

Table B

Group A	[1] child	[2] teenager	[3] adult	[4]
Group B	[1] Monday	[2] Wednesday	[3] Friday	[4]
Group C	[1] morning	[2] evening	[3] night	[4]
Group D	[1] go to school	[2] have lunch	[3] come home	[4]
Group E	[1] yesterday	[2] tomorrow	[3] next weekend	[4]

2 Put the lists of words in order. Add one more item at the end of each list.

0 October / March / June
   March, June, October, (November)

1 third / second / fourth
   _____

2 ask for the bill / look at the menu / order your meal
   _____

3 sometimes / often / rarely
   _____

Listening parts 4 and 5

1 🔊 **37** You will hear a woman, Sally, asking about a women's football team. Listen and complete each question.

AFC Women's Football Club

Name:	AFC Women's Football Club
Training day:	0 _*Thursday*_
Time:	1 _____
Cost:	2 £_____
Contact:	John 3 _____
Phone number:	4 _____

2 🔊 **38** You will hear a man talking about the London Olympic stadium. Listen and complete each question.

The London 2012 Olympic stadium

Distance from London – 0 _____*10*_____ km

Work started – 1 22 _____, 2008

Work finished – 2 _____

First event – celebrity 3 _____

Cost – 4 £_____ million

Capacity – third 5 _____ stadium in the UK

Exam guide: listening – filling in notes

In the KEY listening parts 4 and 5 you must listen to a text and then complete some notes about it. The only difference between the two parts is that part 4 is a conversation between two people while part 5 is a monologue (just one person talking).

- Before you listen look at the form you have to fill in. Look at the title and the questions. This tells you what the listening is about and helps you prepare.

- Look closely at the spaces you have to fill in on the form. You have to fill in each one with a word or a figure (for example, a date, a price or a number). What kind of information do you think is missing?

- You will hear the missing information in the order that it appears on the form. If you miss something, don't worry. You will have a second chance to hear it again.

- Use the first listening to write in as many of the answers as you can. Use the second listening to check these answers and focus on any that are missing.

CONSOLIDATION

LISTENING

1 🔊39 Listen to the conversation. Circle A, B or C.

1 What kind of lesson is Lucy going to the sports centre for?
- A gym
- B rock climbing
- C swimming

2 What is in the bathroom?
- A a hairdryer
- B an MP3 player
- C headphones

3 What is on the living room floor?
- A magazines
- B a games console
- C a docking station

2 🔊39 Listen again. Answer the questions.

0 How long is it until Lucy's lesson starts?
Two hours.

1 Why does she want to go to the sports centre earlier?

_____

_____

2 What does her dad want her to do?

_____

_____

3 What was Lucy's dad doing when he sat on the headphones?

_____

_____

4 Where is Lucy's MP3 player?

_____

_____

5 Where does he want Lucy to help him?

_____

_____

6 Why does he think cutting wood is a good idea for Lucy?

_____

_____

VOCABULARY

3 Unscramble the letters. Write the words.

0 I'd love to go *nagilis*, but I can't swim and I'm scared I might fall in the water. ___*sailing*___

1 We don't all want to listen to your music. Put your *oehadpenhs* on. _____

2 I can't do this sum. Have you got a *alaclutocr*?

_____

3 I tried to play *fogl* once, but I couldn't even hit the ball. _____

4 I can't see anything. Have you got a *corth*?

_____

GRAMMAR

4 Complete the sentences. Use the correct form of the verbs in brackets.

0 They ___*had*___ (have) the accident while they *were programming* (program) the satnav.

1 I _____ (tidy) up my bedroom when I _____ (find) my torch.

2 She _____ (use) the coffee machine when she _____ (burn) her hand.

3 Dad _____ (tell) us to do our homework when we _____ (play) on the game console.

4 I _____ (listen) to my MP3 player when it _____ (stop) working.

5 Circle the correct words.

DAD Hey, Ben, why are you looking so sad?

BEN We lost the match.

DAD You [0] *shouldn't* / *must* worry so much. You [1] *mustn't always* / *don't always* have to win.

BEN Yes, but we never win. We [2] *should* / *don't have to* try to win sometimes. Our coach says we [3] *shouldn't* / *must* try harder. He thinks we [4] *should* / *mustn't* have extra training sessions.

DAD What! You already have three. Is he crazy? I think I [5] *shouldn't* / *have to* have a chat with him.

BEN It's OK, Dad. You [6] *mustn't* / *don't have to* do that. I don't think I want to play for the team anymore.

DAD Come on, Ben, you [7] *shouldn't* / *must* give up so easily.

BEN But you always told me that you [8] *should* / *don't have to* love what you do. I don't even like playing football.

DAD Well, you [9] *must* / *shouldn't* always listen to what I say. Sometimes even I get it wrong.

DIALOGUE

6 Complete the conversation. Use the words in the list.

should | windsurfing | sorry | tell | mean
skiing | fear | doing | what | do

ANNA I'm bored.

DAN You ⁰ _____*should*_____ get yourself a hobby, then.

ANNA Like ¹_____?

DAN Well, maybe you could start doing a sport.

ANNA You ²_____, do some exercise?

DAN Exactly. What about a water sport? Sailing or ³_____, or something like that.

ANNA But I've got aquaphobia – you know, a fear of water.

DAN OK, what about rock-climbing? They ⁴_____ lessons at the gym.

ANNA No, I've got acrophobia.

DAN ⁵_____?

ANNA Acrophobia – it's a ⁶_____ of heights.

DAN Snowboarding? ⁷_____?

ANNA No, I've got chionophobia.

DAN Don't ⁸_____ me – a fear of snow.

ANNA Exactly.

DAN I think you've got lazyitus.

ANNA What's that?

DAN The fear of ⁹_____ any exercise!

READING

7 Read the text. Match the titles with the paragraphs.

0 The prizes [C]   2 Try saying this! [ ]
1 The places [ ]   3 Young and old [ ]

All you need to know about the Olympic Games in 150 words

A London is the only city to hold the Games three times (1908, 1948 and 2012). The USA held them four times but in three different cities.

B At the Paris Games in 1900, there were more athletes than spectators. The oldest athlete ever at the games was Sweden's Oscar Swahn. He won a silver medal in shooting in 1920 at the age of 72. The youngest medal winner was Inge Sorensen from Denmark. She was 12 when she won a bronze medal in swimming.

C In the first modern Olympic Games, in Athens in 1896, there were no gold medals. The winners all got silver medals. In the 1900 Games, the winners got trophies instead of medals. Winners first got gold medals in the 1904 Olympics in St Louis, USA.

D And finally, the longest name for an Olympic champion was Prapawadee Jaroenrattanatarakoon from Thailand. She won a gold medal in weightlifting.

WRITING

8 Choose a sport or a sportsperson that you like. Write a text called 'All you need to know about …' (about 150 words).

- Choose some interesting trivia.
- Try to organise it into three or four short paragraphs.
- Can you do it in 150 words exactly?

GRAMMAR
Comparative adjectives `SB p.86`

1 ★☆☆ Write the comparative form of the adjectives.

0 old   *older*
1 bad   _____
2 beautiful   _____
3 easy   _____
4 expensive   _____
5 good   _____
6 happy   _____
7 interesting   _____
8 nice   _____
9 young   _____

2 ★★☆ Complete the B sentences. Use the comparative form of the adjectives in the A sentences.

0 A Question number 1 is difficult.
   B Yes, it is – but question number 2 is *more difficult*!

1 A Was your laptop expensive?
   B Yes, it was, but the old one was _____.

2 A She's young.
   B Yes, but her sister's _____ than her.

3 A This book's interesting.
   B You're right, but the other one is _____.

4 A Wow – that's a good camera.
   B It's not bad. Actually, I want to buy a _____ one than this!

5 A This film's bad!
   B Yes, but the other one was _____!

3 ★★☆ Complete the sentences. Use the comparative form of the adjectives in brackets.

	Sandra	Justine
Age:	12	13
Height:	1.58	1.56
Does homework:	sometimes	always
English score:	93%	74%

0 Sandra is *younger than* Justine. (young)
1 Sandra is _____ Justine. (tall)
2 Justine is _____ Sandra. (hard-working)
3 Sandra is _____ at English _____ Justine. (good)

4 ★★★ Write comparative sentences using your own ideas. Use the words in brackets to help you.

1 your school / another school in your town (*big / good* …?)
   _____

2 you / your best friend (*old / tall / intelligent* …?)
   _____

3 two TV programmes (*funny / long / exciting* …?)
   _____

4 (any two things you want to compare)
   _____

can / can't for ability `SB p.87`

5 ★☆☆ Look at the pictures. Write a sentence for each picture.

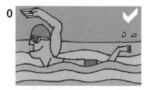

He *can swim*.

He _____

She _____

He _____

6 ★★☆ Write sentences so they are true for you. Use the verbs in the list to help you, or other verbs you know.

~~sing~~ | ~~speak French~~ | walk | run fast
play the guitar | fly | swim

0 I can   *sing* , but I can't *speak French* .
1 I can't _____, but I can _____.
2 My father can _____, but he can't _____.
3 My best friend can _____, but he/she can't _____.
4 Birds can _____, but they can't _____.

Superlative adjectives SB p.88

7 ★☆☆ Complete the conversations. Use the phrases in the list.

~~the laziest~~ | the best | the oldest | the worst
the most expensive | the most interesting
the most difficult

0 **A** Who's *the laziest* kid in your class?

B Steve. He never does anything!

1 **A** That test was hard!

B It was. In fact it was _____ test this year.

2 **A** Do you think they're a good band?

B Yes, I do. They're _____ band around at the moment.

3 **A** That's a great shirt.

B Yes, it's really nice. But I can't buy it. It's _____ shirt in the shop!

4 **A** What a horrible day. Rain, rain, rain.

B Yes, I think it's _____ day of the summer.

5 **A** Who's _____ person in your family?

B Grandpa. He's 74.

6 **A** You really like History, don't you?

B Yes, I think it's _____ subject at school.

8 ★★☆ Circle the correct words.

0 Is the Amazon *longer* / *(the longest)* river in the world?

1 Alex is *taller* / *the tallest* than me.

2 Yesterday was *colder* / *the coldest* day of the year.

3 My father is *younger* / *the youngest* than my mother.

4 He wants to be *richer* / *the richest* person in the country.

5 Is this exercise *more difficult* / *the most difficult* on this page?

9 ★★☆ Complete the sentences. Use the superlative form of the adjectives in the list.

~~rich~~ | boring | delicious | high
fast | important | strong

0 She's got a really big house and a Porsche. She's *the richest* person I know!

1 He can pick up a 50 kilo bag of potatoes. He's _____ man I know.

2 I almost fell asleep in the film. It was _____ film out for a long time!

3 Wow! This fish is so good! It's _____ food that my mother makes!

4 This car does 280 kph. Maybe it's _____ car in the world.

5 Which is _____ mountain in the world?

6 Some people say that the day you get married is _____ day of your life.

10 ★★★ Write one comparative sentence and one superlative sentence about the things in each group, using your own ideas. Use the adjectives in the list to help you.

~~cold~~ | ~~hot~~ | healthy | enjoyable | delicious
fast | cheap | interesting | good | difficult
boring | big

0 winter – summer – autumn

   Summer is hotter than autumn.

   Winter's the coldest time of the year.

1 running – football – swimming

   _____

   _____

2 pizza – chips – salad

   _____

   _____

3 music – films – books

   _____

   _____

4 Brazil – China – Britain

   _____

   _____

5 train – plane – bus

   _____

   _____

GET IT RIGHT!

Comparative and superlative adjectives

We form the comparative of <u>long</u> adjectives with *more* + adjective. We form the comparative of <u>short</u> adjectives (one syllable) with adjective + *-er*. Don't use *more* with adjective + *-er*.

✓ My cousin is **younger** than me.

✗ My cousin is ~~more younger~~ than me.

We form the superlative of <u>long</u> adjectives with (*the*) *most* + adjective. We form the superlative of <u>short</u> adjectives (one syllable) with *the* + adjective + *-est*. Don't use (*the*) *most* with short adjective + *-est*.

✓ It was **the coldest** winter in history.

✗ It was ~~the most coldest winter~~ in history.

Complete the text with the comparative or superlative form of the adjectives in brackets.

I love climbing mountains. For me, it's [1]_____ (exciting) hobby. I think [2]_____ (beautiful) mountains in the world are in New Zealand. But [3]_____ (tall) mountains in the world are in Asia. The mountains in England are [4]_____ (small) than in Asia and the weather is [5]_____ (cold). The USA has [6]_____ (warm) weather than England, but Asia's weather is [7]_____ (hot). So, I love going climbing in Asia.

VOCABULARY

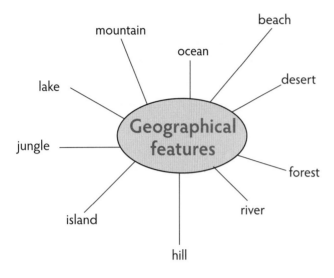

mountain
ocean
beach
lake
desert
jungle
Geographical features
forest
island
river
hill

The weather

cloudy

cold

humid

foggy

freezing

hot

Phrases with *with*

to be **busy with** something
(to have nothing) **to do with** (me)
to **be with** someone
to **be good with** something (e.g. animals / children)
a place **with** (big rooms / lots of animals / lots of tourists)

dry

rainy

Key words in context

attractive	The butterfly is a beautiful blue and red insect – it's very **attractive**.
brave	When the lion attacked the girl, a **brave** man helped her.
courage	I wanted to talk to the President, but I didn't have the **courage**.
dangerous	It's a **dangerous** animal – don't go near it, it might bite you.
extreme	There was a 150 kph wind! That's really **extreme** weather.
ice	Be careful! It was very cold last night and there's **ice** on the roads.
medicine	He was ill so we went to the chemist's to buy some **medicine** for him.
on record	Last night was the coldest night **on record** in this country.
temperature	Sometimes the **temperature** goes up to 37° Celsius.

sunny

warm

wet

windy

Geographical features SB p.86

1 ★★☆ **Match the words and the definitions.**

ᵃforest | ᵇisland | ᶜhill | ᵈdesert | ᵉbeach | ᶠjungle
ᵍocean | ʰriver | ⁱlake | ʲmountain

0 a place with lots of trees growing together `a`

1 an area of sand (or rocks) near the sea ☐

2 a bit of land with water all round it ☐

3 a high bit of land (not as high as a mountain) ☐

4 water that moves across the land and into the sea ☐

5 a very high piece of land ☐

6 a big area of water with land around it ☐

7 a very large area of sea water ☐

8 an area in a hot country with trees and plants close together and wild animals ☐

9 a big, hot, dry area of land (often with sand) ☐

2 ★★★ **Use the words in Exercise 1 to complete the sentences. Make the words plural if you need to.**

0 It's important to take lots of water with you if you go into the _____desert_____.

1 Madagascar is a very big _____ in the Indian Ocean.

2 I love sitting on a _____ and swimming in the sea.

3 The longest _____ in the world is the Nile.

4 The Himalayas has the highest _____ in the world.

5 I was very tired after I cycled up the _____.

6 Let's go for a walk in the _____ and look for wild mushrooms!

7 We took a small boat and went round the _____.

8 Tigers live in the _____ in India and Indonesia.

9 The ship hit a rock and went to the bottom of the _____.

The weather SB p.89

3 ★☆☆ **Complete the 'weather' words with the missing letters.**

1 Yesterday was c _o l d_ but today it's really f _ _ _ zin _! It's a bit w _ _ _ y too.

2 It was nice and w _ _ _ yesterday. But today is even
better: it's s _ _ ny, h _ t and d _ y!

3 It's a horrible day today. It's c _ _ _ dy and cold. This morning it was r _ _ _ y so it's w _ t here, too.

4 When it's f _ _ _ _ _ like today, it's hard to see where you're going!

4 ★★☆ **Use the words in Exercise 3 to complete the text.**

I'm from Britain but I live in Brasilia, the capital of Brazil. The weather here is usually good – the temperature is normally between about 12 degrees and 28 degrees Celcius, so it's never really
⁰____cold____. Some days in summer it's really
¹h_____, but a lot of the time it's just nice and ²w_____, especially in the evenings.

There is one period in the year – from about May to July or August – when it just doesn't rain! So everything is very ³d_____. At other times of the year, the weather can be ⁴r_____ – and when it rains, it rains really hard!

Some days in the morning, when you wake up, the sky is grey and ⁵c_____, but then the clouds go away and the morning can be bright and
⁶s_____.

So, the weather here is quite nice really – not like my home country, Britain, where it's ⁷f_____ some days in winter!

WordWise SB p.91
Phrases with *with*

5 ★☆☆ **Complete the sentences. Use the phrases in the list.**

with 220 bedrooms | busy with
with tomato sauce | good with
to do with you | with you

0 It's a big hotel _with 220 bedrooms_.

1 **A** Isn't Alice here?

  B No. I thought she came _____.

2 It's delicious – pasta _____ and chicken.

3 She looks after my little brother. She's really _____ children.

4 Please don't ask me about it. It's got nothing _____.

5 I phoned him but he didn't answer. He was _____ his homework.

READING

1 REMEMBER AND CHECK Match the phrases to make sentences. Then check your answers in the article on page 85 of the Student's Book.

0	The San people	in small houses	and tell stories about hunting.
1	When they are ill,	near a fire	from the older people.
2	The people in the tribe live	difficult for people and animals	from plants.
3	San children have to learn	San bushmen	with bows and arrows.
4	In the evening, the San people sit	hunt animals	to show them the places and animals.
5	In the Kalahari, life can be	they get medicine	because it's very dry.
6	Tourists to the Kalahari often have	about the dangers around them	made from wood and grass.

2 Read the information. Mark the sentences T (true) or F (false).

0 The Inuit do not move around like they did in the past. `T`

1 The Inuit get their food from hunting and fishing. ☐

2 Inuit houses made of ice are called igloos. ☐

3 A harpoon is a kind of animal. ☐

4 The Inuit still use sledges, but not with dogs. ☐

The Inuit – in the past and nowadays

The Inuit are people who live in the north of Canada, the USA and Greenland, in a place of snow and ice.

	In the past	Nowadays
Living Areas	In the past, the Inuit people lived in camps and they moved all the time, depending on the weather.	Now they live in fixed communities, groups of houses mostly near the sea and at the mouths of rivers.
Homes	The Inuit people lived in tents made from animal skins, or in igloos (traditional houses made of ice).	These days they live in wooden houses that are built in the south of Canada. But they still use tents, too, next to the houses, and igloos when they are hunting.
Clothes	They wore clothes made from the skin or fur of the animals that they killed.	Now the Inuit mostly wear modern, ready-made clothes, but they still also use traditional fur boots, gloves and clothes, especially in the winter.
Food Supply	The Inuit got their food by hunting and fishing, using bows and arrows but also harpoons (special tools for killing fish or seals). They also caught animals that they could eat, using traps.	Now, the Inuit continue to hunt and fish but they usually get their food using guns and modern fishing equipment.
Transport	They had dogs that carried things and that also pulled the sledges for people to move around. On the rivers, they used kayaks (a special boat for one or two people).	Now they use sledges with motors and their boats also have motors. And in the communities, they use cars.

3 Read the text again. Are the facts 1–5 true about only the past, only the present, or both? Tick (✓) the boxes.

		Only the past	Only the present	Both past and present
0	Living in camps	✓	☐	☐
1	Living in igloos	☐	☐	☐
2	Wearing clothes made of fur	☐	☐	☐
3	Using guns	☐	☐	☐
4	Using dogs	☐	☐	☐
5	Using boats	☐	☐	☐

DEVELOPING WRITING

An informal email

1 Read Jake's email to Monika. Answer the questions.

1 Where is Monika going on holiday?

2 Which two places does Jake recommend?

Hey Monika,

Great to get your email yesterday. So, your summer holiday will be in Thailand? That's wonderful! I hope you have a fantastic time.

Maybe you know (or maybe not?) that I went to Thailand two years ago with my family. It's a great place and I enjoyed it a lot. Food, people, places – so different from Europe!

Anyway, I'm writing to give you some ideas. People usually arrive in Bangkok and stay there a few days. Well, when you are in Bangkok, don't miss the Royal Palace! It's just fabulous, I'm attaching a photo I took. You have to go there!

And if you like beaches and swimming and things – and I think you do! – then make sure you go to the Phi Phi Islands. They're in the south of Thailand and you can swim and go diving and see lots of wonderful fish. It's very beautiful there and it's a great place to relax. I'd really recommend it!

Well, I have to go now, but if you want any more ideas, please write to me, OK?

Your friend,

Jake

PS You mustn't forget to take your camera to Thailand, OK!?

---

2 Read Jake's email again. <u>Underline</u> the adjectives that he uses to give his opinion of things in Thailand.

1 Are the adjectives positive or negative?

_____

2 Does Jake use any adjectives that are new for you? Look them up in a dictionary if you need to.

3 Complete the phrases that Jake uses. What is he doing when he writes these things?

0 _____*Don't*_____ miss the Royal Palace.

1 You _____ go there!

2 _____ you go to the Phi Phi Islands.

3 I'd really _____ it.

4 You _____ forget to take your camera!

Pronunciation

Vowel sounds: /ɪ/ and /aɪ/

Go to page 120. 🔊

4 You are going to write an email to an English-speaking friend and tell them about a place that you know and that you really like. (You can imagine that you know the place.) Plan your email. Think about the place you want to write about.

● What is special about it?

● What adjectives do you want to use to describe it?

● What things or places there do you want to recommend to your friend?

● What do you think your friend should take there? And do there?

● How can you start and finish your email?

5 Write your email (about 150–200 words). Make sure that you give your opinion about the place(s) you are talking about. Use Jake's email to help you.

LISTENING

1 🔊43 **Listen to the conversations. Mark the sentences T (true) or F (false).**

CONVERSATION 1

0   The girl wants to go for a walk.   `F`

1   The girl doesn't know what a jigsaw puzzle is.   ☐

2   The girl doesn't want to do a jigsaw puzzle.   ☐

3   It's raining.   ☐

CONVERSATION 2

4   It's a cloudy day.   ☐

5   The boy doesn't want to wear trousers.   ☐

6   The boy likes the girl's T-shirt.   ☐

7   The girl doesn't understand what's written on her T-shirt.   ☐

2 🔊43 **Listen again. Complete the lines from the conversations.**

CONVERSATION 1

BOY   0 _____*What*_____ a horrible day today.

GIRL   Yes, it 1_____ .

BOY   I just thought, well, something different, you know, 2_____ a jigsaw puzzle.

GIRL   I know. What a 3_____ ! On a rainy day like today, it's a nice thing to do!

CONVERSATION 2

BOY   Wow, 4_____ fantastic day. It's so warm and 5_____ !

GIRL   So let's go out 6_____ .

GIRL   Hey, nice 7_____ . They look great.

BOY   Thanks. And I really like your T-shirt – 8_____ colour!

DIALOGUE

1 **Complete the conversation. Use the words in the list.**

~~can~~ | can't | idea | perhaps | maybe | let's

BOY   What a horrible day. It's cold and snowing.

GIRL   I know. What 0_____*can*_____ we do?

BOY   Well, we 1_____ go outside. So, 2_____ do something here.

GIRL   Well, I thought, 3_____ we can watch a film.

BOY   Well, OK, yes. Or 4_____ we could play some computer games.

GIRL   That's a great 5_____ .

2 **Write a conversation for the picture. Use Listening Exercise 2 and Dialogue Exercise 1 to help you.**

_____

_____

_____

_____

_____

PHRASES FOR FLUENCY   SB p.91

1 **Put the conversation in order.**

☐ A   No problem. I'll call Jenny in a minute, she'll probably know.

☐ A   Oh, yes, that's fixed it! Well done. Thank you!

`1` A   Can you help me with my camera? Something's wrong with it and I don't know much about cameras.

☐ A   Oh! So you can't help me, then?

☐ B   Not really. I'm sorry.

☐ B   Good idea. She's really good with these things. Oh – hang on! How about if you press this button here?

☐ B   I don't know much either.

2 **Complete the conversation. Use the phrases in the list.**

~~in a minute~~ | not really | either | then | no problem

A   (on the phone) Hi, John? Sorry, I'm a bit late. But I'll be at your place 0 _*in a minute*_ .

B   1_____ , Steve. Is there a lot of traffic, 2_____ ?

A   3_____ . But I'm cycling and it's raining.

B   Ugh. I hate cycling in the rain!

A   I don't really like it 4_____ . But I haven't got any money for the bus. Anyway, I shouldn't really be cycling and talking on the phone at the same time. So, bye!

Reading and Writing part 7

1 Complete the text. Write one word in each space.

My name (0)_____*is*_____ Alison Davey and I live (1)_____ Alice Springs, Australia. It's not a very big town – only about 25,000 people (2)_____ here.

Alice Springs (most people just call it 'Alice') is in the north (3)_____ the country. It's not a bad place to live (4)_____ it isn't very exciting. There's a nice park that you can visit and outside the town there are some mountains where you can (5)_____ walking.

It's a very hot place and it's very dry too because it doesn't (6)_____ very much.

In January, it's really hot and sometimes the (7)_____ can go up to 36 degrees. Alice is a very long (8)_____ from the sea so there aren't any beaches here.

Right now I'm at school but I want to go to university later. I want to go to Sydney because it's bigger (9)_____ Alice and a bit (10)_____ interesting too!

Exam guide: open cloze

In this kind of exercise, you have to write one word in each space. These exercises test your grammar and vocabulary, but mostly grammar.

- First, read the text from beginning to end without worrying about the spaces. Then you get a good idea of the overall meaning.
- Then, when you go back to the beginning, think about meaning and grammar – for example, in space number 1, you know that people live in a city or town, so the answer is *in*.

- Look at spaces 9 and 10 – what's the word that comes after a comparative adjective like *bigger*? And what's the word that goes before longer adjectives like *interesting*?
- Sometimes you have to think about meaning too. For example, in space 6, the text says that the town is very dry because something doesn't happen very much. What stops a place being dry? That's right – *rain*.

2 Complete the email. Write one word in each space.

Hi Amy,

Well, here we (0)_____*are*_____ at last. Niagara Falls! We flew from London (1)_____ Toronto and then (2)_____ dad hired a car and we drove to see the waterfalls. Wow – it's a fantastic place. I don't think there is anything more beautiful (3)_____ this in the world. I read that Niagara Falls isn't (4)_____ highest waterfall in the world – I think that's the Angel Falls in Venezuela – but it is really big. When you go close, the noise from the water is so loud, you can't (5)_____ other people talking!

We stayed for about two hours. We walked around and took a lot (6)_____ photos. Then we went to the hotel – it's a really small hotel (7)_____ only ten rooms. I'm happy because I've (8)_____ my own room, and my parents are in another room.

Well, we (9)_____ having a great time here. Tomorrow we go back to Toronto. Can I (10)_____ to you again from there?

See you!

Beth

10 | AROUND TOWN

GRAMMAR

be going to for intentions [SB p.94]

1 ★☆☆ **Complete the sentences with the correct form of the verb *to be*. Use the contracted form.**

0   I _'m_ going to buy some stamps at the post office.

1   We _____ going to see a show at the concert hall.

2   I'm taking my children to the sports centre. They _____ going to have a swimming lesson.

3   I'm going to the shopping mall to meet my wife. She _____ going to take me for lunch.

4   We're going to the bus station. We _____ going to catch the number 51 home.

2 ★★☆ **Complete the questions, then match them with the answers. Use the verbs in brackets.**

0   _Are_ you going _to watch_ the game? (watch)

1   _____ they going _____ in a hotel? (stay)

2   _____ we going _____ Gran this weekend? (visit)

3   _____ Dave going _____ a taxi? (take)

4   _____ Jo going _____ the competition? (enter)

5   _____ Katie going _____ tonight? (cook)

a   ☐ No, they're not. They're going camping.

b   ☐ No, he's going to walk there.

c   ☐ Yes, she is. She's going to win!

d   ☐ I hope so. I'm so tired.

e   ☐ 0 ☐ Yes, I am. I love football.

f   ☐ Yes, we are. We're going to go on Sunday.

3 ★★☆ **Complete the answers with *going to* and the verbs in brackets.**

What ⁰_are you going to do_ (do) when you leave school?

A   'I ¹_____ (study) Maths at Nottingham University. Two of my friends ²_____ (go) there too so we ³_____ (find) a house and live in it together.'

B   'I'm not sure. My best friend ⁴_____ (travel) around the world and he wants me to go with him. I ⁵_____ (not do) that – I haven't got enough money – but I ⁶_____ (not go) to university either.

4 ★★★ **Write five plans you have for this year. Use *going to*.**

I'm going to ... _____

_____

_____

_____

Present continuous for arrangements [SB p.95]

5 ★★☆ **Look at Claire's diary. Complete the sentences with the present continuous form of the verbs in brackets.**

	Morning	Afternoon	Evening
Monday		tennis – Sue	kids – cinema
Tuesday	breakfast with Tim		
Wednesday			party at Jo's
Thursday	meeting with Jen	dentist – 4 pm	
Friday	golf		fly to Rome

0   Claire and Sue _are playing_ (play) tennis on Monday afternoon.

1   Claire _____ (fly) to Rome on Friday evening.

2   Claire _____ (go) to Jo's party on Wednesday evening.

3   Claire _____ (go) to the dentist on Thursday afternoon.

4   Claire and Tim _____ (have) breakfast on Tuesday morning.

5   Claire _____ (play) golf on Friday morning.

6   Claire and her children _____ (go) to the cinema on Monday evening.

7   Claire and Jen _____ (have) a meeting on Thursday morning.

6 ★★★ Write the questions for the answers about Claire. Use the present continuous of the verbs.

0 *Is Claire going to the dentist on Thursday?*
Yes, she is. Her appointment is at 4 pm.

1 _____
No, they're having breakfast.

2 _____
No, she's flying in the evening.

3 _____
Yes, but they don't know what film to see yet.

4 _____
That's right. They're playing in the afternoon.

7 ★★☆ Mark the sentences P (present arrangement) or F (future arrangement).

0 Henry's not at home. He's fishing with his dad. | P |
1 Sorry, I can't help you. I'm studying. | |
2 Are you doing anything this evening? | |
3 Look at the baby! She's trying to walk. | |
4 Is Aunt Mary coming to stay next week? | |
5 We're looking at new houses this afternoon. | |
6 I'm staying at my friend's house tonight. | |

8 ★★★ Write five arrangements you have for this weekend. Use the present continuous.

Adverbs SB p.97

9 ★☆☆ Read the sentences. Write the names under the pictures.

Bella paints really well.
Molly paints quite badly.
Tim rides his bike dangerously.
Ben rides his bike carefully.

0 *Molly*   1 _____

2 _____   3 _____

10 ★★☆ Unscramble the words to make adjectives. Then write the adverb form.

		adjective	adverb
0	saye	*easy*	*easily*
1	wols		
2	kiquc		
3	souranged		
4	revosun		
5	teiqu		
6	dab		
7	larefuc		
8	dogo		

11 ★★★ Circle the correct words.

0 Jackson played very good / well, and won the match easy / easily.
1 It was an easy / easily test and I finished it really quick / quickly.
2 My dad isn't a very careful / carefully driver and sometimes he drives quite dangerous / dangerously.
3 Please be quiet / quietly in the library – you can talk, but not too loud / loudly.
4 I didn't do good / well in the test – I had a really bad / badly day.
5 He's quite a nervous / nervously person and he talks really quiet / quietly.

GET IT RIGHT! ◉

Adverbs usually come immediately after the object of the sentence or after the verb (if there is no object). They never come between the verb and the object.

✓ He drives his car dangerously.
✗ He drives dangerously his car.

Change the adjective in brackets into an adverb and put it in the correct place in the sentence.

0 He can run fast, but he can't swim. (good)
He can run fast, but he can't swim well.

1 You should drive when it's raining. (careful)
_____

2 She speaks French and German. (fluent)
_____

3 She was walking because she was late for school. (quick)
_____

4 They did the homework because they worked together. (easy)
_____

VOCABULARY

Places in town

- bus station
- concert hall
- football stadium
- car park
- police station
- opera house
- shopping mall
- post office
- harbour
- sports centre
- skyscraper
- castle

Things in a town

zebra crossing

youth club

speed camera

graffiti wall

cycle lane

litter bin

billboard

high street

skateboard park

Key words in context

culture	I love meeting people from different **cultures** – there's so much you can learn from them.
population	The **population** of our town is about 20,000.
local	Our **local** shop is just across the road from our house.
invite	The Jacksons **invited** us to dinner at their house.
tourism	**Tourism** is very important for our country. Millions of people visit us each year.
pedestrian	**Pedestrians** must be careful when they cross the road.
fluent	He speaks really good French. He's almost **fluent**.
tourist attraction	The museum is a really big **tourist attraction**. Lots of people visit it.
sand	We went to the beach and now I've got **sand** in my hair.
mine	This **mine** goes more than 200 m under the ground.
diamond	Is that a **diamond** ring? Wow, it's beautiful.
resort	Cannes is a popular **resort** in the south of France.
demolish	They **demolished** the old stadium because they want to build a new one.

Places in a town SB p.94

1 ★★★ **Complete the words. Use the picture clues to help you.**

0 concert hall

1 b _ s st _ t _ _ n

2 f _ _ tb _ ll st _ d _ _ m

3 c _ r p _ rk

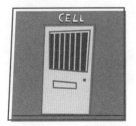

4 p _ l _ c _ st _ t _ _ n

5 p _ st _ ff _ c _

6 sp _ _ rts c _ ntr _

2 ★★★ **Complete the text. Use the words in Exercise 1.**

Our town is great. It's got everything I need. There's a really good sports ⁰ _centre_ . You can do lots of different sports. There's a big ¹_____ hall as well and I often go to see my favourite bands there. Most Saturdays I go to the football ²_____ to see our football team play. There's a really big shopping ³_____ with lots of shops in it. And if you ever get bored, you can go to the bus ⁴_____ to catch a bus and visit another town.

3 ★★★ **Where are these people? Choose from the places in Exercise 1.**

0 'What time does the swimming pool close?' _sports centre_

1 'I want to send this letter to Australia.' _____

2 'I think Manchester United are going to win today.'

_____

3 'What time is the next bus to Liverpool?'

_____

4 'I want to buy some new shoes.' _____

5 'The band start playing at 8 pm.' _____

6 'It costs £2 every hour we stay.' _____

7 'There's a problem at the bank. Come quickly.'

_____

Things in town SB p.97

4 ★★★ **Write compound nouns using the nouns in the lists.**

~~cycle~~ | graffiti | speed | zebra | bill | litter
~~lane~~ | board | camera | crossing | bin | wall

0 _cycle lane_   3 _____
1 _____   4 _____
2 _____   5 _____

5 ★★★ **Match the words from Exercises 1 and 4 to the definitions.**

0 Cars slow down for this. _speed camera_

1 You find lots of shops here. _____

2 You can ride your bike safely here. _____

3 It advertises things on the side of the road.

_____

4 Use this to cross the road safely. _____

5 A great place for local artists to paint. _____

6 A good place for young people to meet and have fun. _____

7 Throw your rubbish in this. _____

6 ★★★ **Which of these sentences are true about your town? Correct the ones that are false.**

1 Cars always stop at zebra crossings.

2 There are lots of things for young people to do. There are graffiti walls and a really good youth club.

3 Speed cameras make the roads safer.

4 You can get everywhere on your bike using cycle lanes.

5 People always use the litter bins to throw away rubbish.

6 There are lots of billboards.

7 The high street is full of shoppers at the weekend.

READING

1 **REMEMBER AND CHECK** What are these things? Check your answers in the blogs on page 93 of the Student's Book.

0 The Burj al Arab

A building in Dubai that looks like a ship's sail.

1 Jebel Ali

_____

2 khaliji

_____

3 Yellowknife

_____

4 Snowking Winter Festival

_____

2 Read the article. Write the names of the towns under the pictures.

1 _____

2 _____

3 _____

4 _____

UNUSUAL TOWNS

Monowi, USA

Elsie Eiler is famous in the town of Monowi in Nebraska and everybody knows her name. That's because Elsie is the only person who lives there. Monowi was never a big town. In the 1930s the population was 150 but over the years people slowly started leaving. In 2000 there were only two people left; Elsie and her husband, Rudy. When Rudy died, Elsie became the only citizen.

Thames Town, China

Shanghai is one of China's biggest cities. But just outside of Shanghai is a rather unusual town called Thames Town. It cost £500 million to build and it is part of their 'One City, Nine Towns' project. When you walk down the streets there you might forget you are in China. You might start thinking you are in England.

That is because Thames Town is a copy of an English town. The streets and the buildings all look English. It has red phone boxes, London street signs, fish and chip shops and English pubs. There are also statues of Harry Potter and James Bond. Elsewhere in China, you can find the Eiffel Tower, an Austrian village and even Stonehenge.

Sheffield, Australia

In the 1980s, the citizens of Sheffield on the Australian island of Tasmania decided they wanted more tourists to visit their town. They had an idea to turn their streets into an outdoor art gallery. They asked artists to paint huge paintings on the walls around town. Children from the local school helped too. They painted little murals on the rubbish bins. There are now more than 60 of these murals, which show important scenes from history.

The plan worked and these days about 200,000 people visit Sheffield every year.

Roswell, USA

Some people believe that in 1947 an alien spacecraft crashed near the town of Roswell in New Mexico. They believe that the American military seized this UFO and took it to a secret place outside of the town. These days Roswell sees many tourists who are interested in life on other planets. There are many shops that sell souvenirs and there is one fast food restaurant with a UFO theme. There is also a museum about aliens.

3 Read the article again. Write the names of the towns after the sentences.

0 Are there aliens here? *Roswell*

1 They wanted more people to visit here. _____

2 It has a population of one. _____

3 It's near to a really big city. _____

4 People didn't want to live here. _____

5 It's like being in another country. _____

6 It's a mysterious place. _____

7 It's a great place if you like art. _____

DEVELOPING WRITING

An informal letter / email

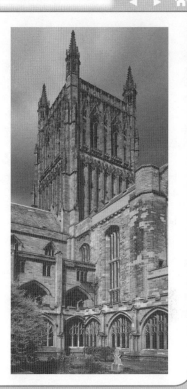

Hi Jessie,

Thanks for your letter and all your news. Sorry about your broken arm – what a terrible thing to happen. I hope you feel better soon. Just be careful when you get back on your bike!

Anyway, I'm sorry my reply is a bit late, but there's so much happening it's difficult to find any free time.

The move here was OK. The new house is nice and big. I've finally got my own bedroom. Worcester is quite a small town (well, compared to Manchester) but it seems quite nice. There are lots of good shops on the High Street and there are a few parks to hang out in. I'm sending you a photo of the cathedral. It's a really beautiful building. I'm spending most of my time at the sports centre. I'm quite fit at the moment. I haven't got any friends here yet but I'm starting school on Monday. I'm sure I'll find some. I'm feeling a bit nervous.

Anyway, I miss you loads, of course. I can't wait to hear all your news. Please give my love to everyone, especially Tom and Jasmine. By the way, Mum says we're going to visit next month so I hope I'll see you all soon. Hope everything's OK.

Lots of love,

Olivia

---

1 **Read the email. Answer the questions.**

0 How did Jessie break her arm?

She fell off her bike.

1 Where is Olivia living now?

_____

2 Where did she live?

_____

3 How does Olivia feel about starting school?

_____

2 **Read the email again. Write the expressions that mean:**

1 I was sad to hear about …

_____

2 I think about you a lot.

_____

3 Please write to me soon.

_____

4 Say hello to …

_____

Writing tip: an informal letter / email

We usually write informal letters to family and friends to keep in touch and pass on our news. These days most people do this with emails.

- Use informal, friendly language.
- If you are writing a reply to a letter, don't forget to react to your friend's news. We usually do this in our opening paragraph.
- Always ask how the person you are writing to is. You can do this at the beginning or the end of your letter.
- Use the main paragraph of the letter to give your news.

3 **Write an informal letter to a friend (about 120–150 words). Choose one of these situations.**

- Your pen friend wants to know more about the town where you live. Write and tell them.
- You're going to move house. Write to your friend to give them the news and tell them a bit about the town.
- You are spending the holiday with your aunt and uncle. Write to your friend and tell them about the town where you are staying.

LISTENING

1 ◀»44 Listen to the conversations. Complete the table.

	Invitation accepted	Invitation not accepted
Conversation 1	☐	☐
Conversation 2	☐	☐
Conversation 3	☐	☐

2 ◀»44 Listen again. Complete the sentences.

Kate and Jim
Kate invites Jim to ^{0} _the sports centre_ .
He says ^{1}_____ because
^{2}_____.

Ian and Ruth
Ian invites Ruth to ^{3}_____ on
^{4}_____.
She offers to pay for ^{5}_____.
He says the tickets are ^{6}_____.

Dan and Anna
Dan invites Anna to ^{7}_____ at
^{8}_____.
She is ^{9}_____ until
^{10}_____.
They arrange to meet ^{11}_____.

DIALOGUE

1 ◀»44 Put the first two conversations in order. Then listen again and check.

1 | 1 | KATE | Do you want to go to the sports centre later? |

☐ KATE OK, maybe next week then.

☐ KATE What about tomorrow?

☐ JIM No, I'm busy all week.

☐ JIM Let's see.

☐ JIM I'm sorry. I can't. I'm busy.

2 ☐ IAN It's *Madam Butterfly*. I've got tickets right at the front.

☐ IAN No, it's a present from me.

☐ IAN Well, you deserve it.

☐ IAN Would you like to go to the opera house with me on Saturday?

☐ RUTH That would be great. What's the opera?

☐ RUTH Wow. How much were they? You must let me pay for mine.

☐ RUTH That's really kind of you.

2 Write two short conversations. Use these situations.

Conversation 1
- Boy invites girl to cinema.
- She says yes.
- They agree on a time.

Conversation 2
- Girl invites boy to party.
- He asks what day and when.
- He can't make it and says why.

▰ TRAIN TO THiNK ▰

Problem solving

1 The town council has money to build one new building. Look at the first three suggestions and match the advantages and disadvantages to each one.

~~good to get bands into town~~
bad for shops on high street
create lots of jobs
stop people parking on street
could bring more cars into town
could be noisy at night

Suggestions	Advantages	Disadvantages
concert hall	*good to get bands into town*	
shopping mall		
car park		

2 Think of an advantage and a disadvantage for these three suggestions.

Suggestions	Advantages	Disadvantages
football stadium		
bus station		
sports centre		

3 Complete the statement. Use your own ideas.

I think the _____ is the best idea
because _____
and _____.

Pronunciation

Voiced /ð/ and unvoiced /θ/ consonants
Go to page 121.   ◀»

96

CAMBRIDGE ENGLISH: Key

Reading and Writing part 4

1   Read the article about Shanghai. Are sentences 1–4 'Right' (A) or 'Wrong' (B)? If there isn't enough information to answer 'Right' or 'Wrong', choose 'Doesn't say' (C).

Mini-Shanghai

It's difficult to know exactly how many people live in the Chinese city of Shanghai, but it's at least 20 million. For sure, it's one of the world's biggest cities. Of course, you need a lot of space to find room for so many people, and to give you an idea of just how big Shanghai is, there is a model of the whole city on the third floor of Shanghai's Urban Planning Museum. The model is huge. It's 93 m² and it covers the whole floor of the museum. In fact, it's too big to take a photograph of the whole thing. You can try but you'll find you have to take quite a few photos.

Of course, Shanghai is a city that is growing fast and every year there are about 200 new skyscrapers. The model does not show what Shanghai looks like now. It shows Shanghai in the year 2020.

0   The population of Shanghai is more than 20 million.
   (A) Right   B Wrong   C Doesn't say
1   The model is on the top floor of the museum.
   A Right   B Wrong   C Doesn't say
2   You are not allowed to take photos of the model.
   A Right   B Wrong   C Doesn't say
3   The model shows Shanghai in the future.
   A Right   B Wrong   C Doesn't say
4   The model city is a popular tourist attraction.
   A Right   B Wrong   C Doesn't say

Exam guide: right, wrong or doesn't say

In the KEY Reading and Writing part 4 you must read a text and then decide if the information in some sentences about the text is right or wrong. Sometimes there isn't enough information to decide, and for these sentences you should choose the 'Doesn't say' option.

- Read through the text quickly to get an idea of what it is about. Then read a second time, more slowly.
- Read through the questions. Can you answer any of them immediately? Check in the text to make sure you have the correct answer.
- For each question, find the part of the text it refers to. Use the key words in the question to help you find the correct part of the text. For example, in question 0 the words 20 million are there in the first sentence of the text. This is the part of the text you need to look at.

- If you can't find any information to decide if the question is right or wrong, this probably means the text 'doesn't say'. For example, question 1 says the model is on the top floor of the museum. In the text it says it's on the third floor. We don't know how many floors the museum has. The third floor might be the top floor but we can't be sure. We have to choose the 'Doesn't say' option here.
- The order of the questions is the same as the order of the information in the text.

2   Read Jenny's article about moving home. Are sentences 1–5 'Right' (A) or 'Wrong' (B)? If there isn't enough information to answer 'Right' or 'Wrong', choose 'Doesn't say' (C).

A move to the countryside

For the first twelve years of my life my family lived in a large city. Two years ago my parents decided to move to the countryside. I was horrified. How could I leave all my friends? How could I live somewhere with no cinema, with no skateboard park, where the nearest shop was more than 3 km away?

But Mum and Dad didn't listen to me. They were tired of the city life. Mum's a writer so she can live anywhere and Dad looks after me and my two younger brothers. They thought the country was a better place to bring up children.

Well, two years later and I agree with them. I love it here. I love the freedom of being outside. You can ride your bike everywhere. You don't have to worry about cars. Of course, I found new friends. Not as many as I had, but that isn't a problem. I'm still in contact with my very best friend from the city, Anna, and she comes to visit most holidays. She loves it here. She wants her parents to move too.

0   Jenny is 13 years old.
   A Right   (B) Wrong   C Doesn't say
1   Jenny wasn't happy with the idea of moving to the countryside.
   A Right   B Wrong   C Doesn't say
2   Jenny's mum works for a newspaper.
   A Right   B Wrong   C Doesn't say
3   There are five people in Jenny's family.
   A Right   B Wrong   C Doesn't say
4   Jenny has got more friends now.
   A Right   B Wrong   C Doesn't say
5   Jenny went to school with Anna when she lived in the city.
   A Right   B Wrong   C Doesn't say

CONSOLIDATION

LISTENING

1 ◀🔊46 **Listen to the conversations.** (Circle) **A, B or C.**

1 What kind of holiday is Emma going to suggest to her parents?
   A hotel   B houseboat   C camping

2 Who's got the best idea about what they can do?
   A Mike   B Dad   C Mum

3 When are Emma and her family going on holiday?
   A 4 July   B 18 July   C 8 August

2 ◀🔊46 **Listen again. Answer the questions.**

0 Why don't Mike and Emma want to go to the same hotel as last year?

   They think it would be boring.

1 What does Emma think about a camping holiday?
   _____

2 What does Dad think about Emma's suggestion of a holiday on a houseboat?
   _____

3 What is Mum going to suggest to her and her husband's parents?
   _____

4 Mum makes a joke. What does she say?
   _____

5 How soon are Emma and her family going on their holiday?
   _____

VOCABULARY

3 (Circle) **the correct words.**

Before you go on a holiday, you need to think carefully about where you want to go. If you decide to go to a place in the 0(mountains) / beach, for example, you have to know that the weather can be 1freezing / hot (even in summer), and it can also be quite 2windy / warm.

Everybody knows that deserts have 3dry / wet weather, but people sometimes forget that a 4beach / forest holiday means you are close to a lot of water, so the air can be quite 5dry / humid. During the summer months, this can mean that it can get too 6hot / cold, and not everybody likes that. Here are my family's plans for our next holiday: First we're going to 7spend / spending two weeks at a 8hill / lake. Then, on the 1 September, we are 9leaving / leave for a weekend in the mountains.

4 **Complete the sentences. Use the words in the list.**

~~concert hall~~ | post office | cycle lane | billboards
litter bin | speed camera | zebra crossing

0 I can't believe we can't get tickets for the show. There's room for 2,000 people in the _concert hall_.

1 I need some stamps. Can you go to the _____ for me?

2 Careful – don't drive so fast! There's a _____ ahead, so keep to 50 kph, OK?

3 I want to throw this paper away. Is there a _____ around here?

4 Did you see that driver?! There was someone on the _____ and he didn't stop!

5 There's a new _____ that goes along the beach! It's great – we ride along it on Sundays.

6 He's a professional photographer. His photos are on all the _____ at the moment.

GRAMMAR

5 (Circle) **the correct words.**

LILY   When are you going on holiday?

OLIVER   Next weekend. And we are all looking forward to it. It's going to be the 0more / (most) relaxing time of the year!

LILY   That place on the coast where you are staying, is it 1hotter / hottest than it is here?

OLIVER   Not really. It's 2more cold / colder than it is here, and there's usually 3more / most wind. So the temperature is normally five or six degrees lower 4more / than here.

LILY   And it's the world's 5more / most attractive coast.

OLIVER   Do you think so? Well, it's 6more / most beautiful than other places, but we can't swim in the ocean.

LILY   Can't you?

OLIVER   No, the water temperature is just too cold. And I don't think it's 7safe / safely.

LILY   Oh, really. Are there any 8dangerous / dangerously fish?

OLIVER   I don't think there are. But the waves are really high because of the wind. You'd need to swim really 9good / well to go in. But then you'd come out 10quick / quickly again.

DIALOGUE

6 **Complete the conversation. Use the phrases in the list.**

going to go | going to come | can't go | I'd
no problem | like to | busy with | be with me
are going to | you like to

EVA Jack, I'm ⁰ _going to go_ to the concert on Saturday. Would ¹_____ come along? My friend Nick ²_____, so I've got a ticket if you want it.

JACK Saturday? I'm sorry, I can't. I'm ³_____ a project.

EVA I see. Well, maybe another time.

JACK Yeah, thanks for asking. Oh, would you and Nick ⁴_____ come over to our place next Sunday, maybe? We can sit in the garden, and enjoy the beautiful weather. Gavin and Claire ⁵_____ come too.

EVA ⁶_____ love to. That would be great. Let me talk to Nick. I know he's going to visit some relatives on Saturday, but I think he's ⁷_____ back on Sunday morning. So it should be fine. Can I tell you this evening?

JACK ⁸_____. Talk to Nick first, and give me a ring any time.

(later, on the phone)

JACK Hello?

EVA Oh, hi, Jack. It's about next Sunday. I'm really sorry. Nick won't ⁹_____ on Sunday. He's coming back after 7 in the evening, so I'm going to come alone.

JACK OK.

READING

7 **Read the magazine article about Peru. Circle the correct endings (A or B) for each sentence.**

0 Peru is a very popular holiday place …
   A because it offers tourists a lot of attractions.
   B but the weather is often not very good.

1 A holiday on the coast in summer is good …
   A if you like hot and dry weather.
   B if you don't mind a lot of foggy and rainy days.

2 In the Andes, in winter …
   A it's usually foggy, and not very cold.
   B it's usually dry, and it can be very, very cold.

3 In the east of the country there are no mountains …
   A and the weather doesn't change much throughout the year.
   B and there are extreme differences between summer and winter.

So many kinds of weather!

Peru isn't just a beautiful country. Tourists love it because of its attractive jungles, its stunning beaches and the fantastic Peruvian food. And many people come to see Machu Picchu, a very interesting Inca site that's more than 500 years old. But Peru is also famous for its many different climates. If you travel from one place to another, you can have very different weather on the same day!

The weather on the coast is usually dry and warm, often hot. In the summer, it's hardly ever rainy there. In winter, the coast is often foggy, and the fog even has its own name, *garúa*. In the areas near the ocean, the so-called 'rainy season' starts around late May and comes to an end in October.

In the mountains, the famous Andes, it's often cool, and sometimes cold. The summers there are usually rainy, but the winters are very dry, and can be freezing. In the east, where there are no mountains, the weather is usually hot and humid all year round.

WRITING

8 **Write a paragraph about the weather in your country (about 80–100 words). Think about these questions.**

- Is the weather the same all over the country, or are there differences?
- If the weather is different, can you say why?
- What times of the year are good for tourists who want to visit your country?

11 FUTURE BODIES

GRAMMAR

will / won't for future predictions `SB p.104`

1 ★☆☆ **Put the words in order to make sentences.**

0 'll / home / by / I / 7.30. / be
   I'll be home by 7.30.

1 Sunday / home / and / we / stay / at / relax. / On / 'll
   _____

2 come round / you / to / place / Will / tomorrow? / my
   _____

3 you? / I / to / know / where / find / Will
   _____

4 come / the / party. / to / won't / Sebastian
   _____

2 ★★☆ **Complete the sentences. Use the will future form of the verbs. Then match sentences 1–5 to sentences a–f.**

0 | e | Don't worry. I'm sure you _won't have_ problems with the test. (not have)

1 | ☐ | This year at school _____ cool. (be)

2 | ☐ | I'm not sure a picnic is such a great idea.

3 | ☐ | Kate's not sure if she _____ to the cinema tonight. (go)

4 | ☐ | Ben and Mason _____ back from their trip soon. (be)

5 | ☐ | Don't try to repair your bike without me.

a Our teachers _____ probably _____ us to a youth camp in the last week before the holidays. (take)

b Perhaps she _____ at home and work on her project. (stay)

c It _____ probably _____ raining later today. (start)

d I'm sure they _____ lots of stories to tell. (have)

e You always study hard.

f We _____ it together. (do) That _____ much more fun. (be)

3 ★★☆ **Complete the questions. Use the will future form of the verbs in the list.**

~~learn~~ | get married | have | go | have | live

0 When __will__ you __learn__ to drive?

1 _____ you ever _____ in another country?

2 _____ you ever _____ a sports car?

3 How many children _____ you _____?

4 When do you think you _____?

5 _____ you _____ to university after school?

4 ★★★ **Complete the answers. Use the will future form of the verbs in the list. Then match them with the questions in Exercise 3.**

~~have~~ | drive | live | get | take | do

0 I _'ll have_ lots. I love children. | 3 |

1 I think I _____ in Japan for a year before I go to university. | ☐ |

2 A sports car? No. I don't think I _____ ever even _____ a car. | ☐ |

3 I think _____ the driving test before I go to university. | ☐ |

4 I really don't know but I'm sure I _____ married for a long time. | ☐ |

5 Yes, I think I _____ that but I'm not sure what I want to study yet. | ☐ |

5 ★★★ **Answer the questions from Exercise 3 so they are true for you. Use the will future form of the verbs.**

_____
_____
_____
_____
_____

Pronunciation

The /h/ consonant sound
Go to page 121.

First conditional `SB p.106`

6 ★☆☆ **Match each picture with two sentences.**

0   I won't have a lot of money left if I buy it.   **B**

1   If he isn't careful, he'll break them.   ☐

2   The neighbours will get angry if he doesn't stop.   ☐

3   If I buy one of those, I won't be hungry any more.   ☐

4   If he doesn't get up now, he'll be late for school.   ☐

5   If he doesn't practise, he'll never play in a band.   ☐

7 ★★☆ **Complete the sentences. Circle the most likely options.**

0	He won't pass the test	**a** if he doesn't study hard.
		b if he studies hard.
1	I'm sure all of your friends will come to your party	a if you don't invite them.
		b if you invite them.
2	It's raining. If you don't put on your hat,	a you'll get wet.
		b you won't get wet.
3	She'll book a trip to Rome	a if it isn't too expensive.
		b if it's too expensive.
4	If we don't play better,	a we'll win the match.
		b we'll lose the match.
5	If I find another of those T-shirts,	a I won't get one for you.
		b I'll get one for you.

8 ★★☆ **Complete the sentences. Use the first conditional form of the verbs in brackets.**

0   If you _don't listen_ (not listen), your teacher _won't tell_ (not tell) you what to do again.

1   If we _____ (not feed) the cat, she _____ (be) very hungry.

2   The police _____ (stop) him if he _____ (not slow down).

3   If we _____ (take) a map with us, we _____ (find) the way home.

4   Nobody _____ (like) them if they _____ (behave) like that.

5   If Susie _____ (not help) me, I _____ (be) in trouble.

9 ★★★ **Complete the sentences. Use what you think might be the consequences of these situations.**

50 years from now …

1   If scientists invent cars that run without petrol, _____.

2   If time travel becomes possible, _____.

3   If there are 10 billion people on earth, _____.

4   If computers can speak all languages, _____.

5   If people can fly to Mars in 24 hours, _____.

Time clauses with *when / as soon as* `SB p.107`

10 ★★★ **Read the sentences. Circle the correct words.**

0   When we *arrive* / *'ll arrive*, we *send* / *'ll send* you a text message.

1   He *look* / *'ll look* for the book as soon as he *'s* / *'ll be* home.

2   We *watch* / *'ll watch* the film as soon as the electricity *comes* / *will come* back on.

3   As soon I *get* / *'ll get* the money, I *pay* / *'ll pay* you back.

4   I *take* / *'ll take* you to the new museum when you *come* / *'ll come* and see us.

5   Dad *returns* / *will return* from the US as soon as his job there *is* / *will be* finished.

GET IT RIGHT!
First conditional

We use the present simple in the *if* clause and *will* / *won't* in the <u>result</u> clause. We never use *will* / *won't* in the *if* clause.

✓ **If I see** Rory, **I'll tell** him the news.

✗ If I will see Rory, I'll tell him the news.

Find four incorrect uses of *will*. Correct them.

I don't know what to do! I feel ill, but if I won't go to school tomorrow, I'll miss the test. If I'll miss the test, I'll have to do it in the holidays. But if I will go to school and do the test when I'm ill, I'm sure I won't get a good mark. I won't be able to go to London in the holiday if I will have to do the test then. What a difficult decision!

VOCABULARY

Parts of the body

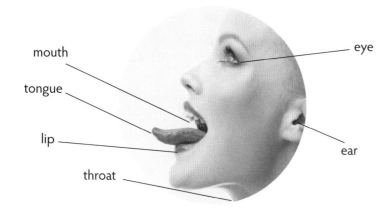

mouth
tongue
lip
throat
eye
ear

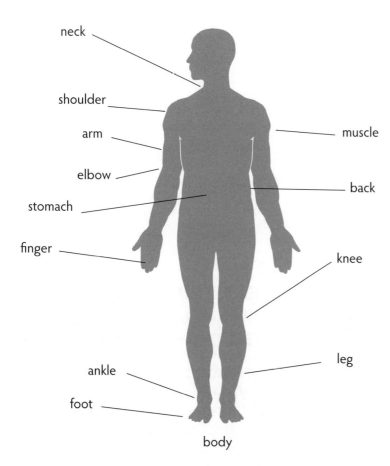

neck
shoulder
arm
elbow
stomach
finger
muscle
back
knee
leg
ankle
foot

body

Aches

stomach ache

ear ache

headache

toothache

when / if

When we arrive, John will prepare some food. (It is certain we will arrive.)

If we arrive before 10, John will prepare some food. (It isn't certain we will arrive before 10.)

Key words in context

fresh air	Let's go outside. I need a bit of **fresh air**.
keep fit	She runs three times a week to **keep fit**.
hurt	Careful! You could **hurt** yourself.
fall	Thomas had a very bad **fall**. He fell down the stairs.
break a leg	I **broke a leg** when I was ten.
see in the dark	I can't **see very well in the dark** so I don't drive at night.
stressed	He seems a bit **stressed**. He's usually not so nervous.
shout at someone	Don't **shout at me**. It wasn't my fault.

Expressions with *do*

do exercise
do the cleaning
do the cooking
do homework
do OK
do well
do (food / drink, in a café, restaurant, etc.)
do (12 kilometres to the litre)

Parts of the body `SB p.104`

1 ★☆☆ **Unscramble the words to make parts of the body.**

~~alenk~~ | bolwe | ilp | elusmc
asmotch | tatroh | enek

0 _____ankle_____

1 _____

2 _____

3 _____

4 _____

5 _____

6 _____

2 ★★☆ **Complete the sentences. Use words for parts of the body.**

0 When he tried to put his shoe on his f _oot_ , he noticed that his a _nkle_ hurt.

1 This rucksack is so heavy that all the m_____ in my n_____ and my s_____ hurt.

2 I've got a lot of pain all up my left arm. It hurts from the ends of my f_____, through my h_____, and up to my e_____.

3 I walked straight into a window. My whole face really hurts; my l_____, my m_____, my e_____ and my e_____ – they all hurt!

4 I ate too much. I've got a s_____ ache.

3 ★★☆ **Write verbs or phrases that match the parts of the body. How many can you find?**

foot – _run, walk,_ _____

mouth – _eat,_ _____

ear – _listen to music,_ _____

arm – _____

eye – _____

fingers – _____

tongue – _____

when and if `SB p.107`

4 ★☆☆ (Circle) **the correct words.**

0 Mum doesn't know when she'll be back. She'll phone us (if) / when she has to work late.

1 I can't do that now. I'll try to do it tomorrow if / when I've got time.

2 I'm not sure where my camera is right now. I'll give it to you if / when I find it.

3 It's still dark outside. We'll start in an hour, if / when it's light.

4 It's Jane's birthday on Sunday. She'll be sad if / when you don't give her a present.

5 I'm writing the email now. I'll be with you in a few minutes if / when I finish.

WordWise `SB p.109`
Expressions with do

5 ★☆☆ **Match the sentences with the pictures.**

0 Let's go in there. They do great food. `e`

1 I'm happy to do the cooking, but it seems we need to go shopping first. ☐

2 I think we need to do some cleaning here. ☐

3 This has the latest technology. It does 30 kilometres to the litre. ☐

4 And Dad thinks I'm doing my homework. Ha ha ha! ☐

5 He isn't doing very well at the moment. I don't think he can give a speech today. ☐

6 ★★☆ **Complete the questions. Use the words in the list.**

~~exercise~~ | ice cream | well | cooking | homework

0 A How often do you do _exercise_ in a week?
  B I run on Mondays and Wednesdays, and go to the gym on Fridays.

1 A Did you do _____ in your last English test?
  B Yes, I got top marks.

2 A Who does the _____ in your family?
  B My dad. He loves it. He thinks he's a chef.

3 A Who does the best _____ in your town?
  B There's an Italian place on my street. It's wonderful.

4 A When do you usually do your _____?
  B Straight after school, when I can still remember everything.

7 ★★★ **Answer the questions in Exercise 6 so they are true for you.**

READING

1 REMEMBER AND CHECK **Complete the sentences. Check your answers in the article on page 103 of the Student's Book.**

0   Because of the food we eat, we'll probably be _taller_ in the future.

1   If we continue doing less physical work, our _____ will get _____.

2   We can expect our legs to get _____, our feet to get _____, and our fingers to get _____.

3   We'll do a lot of computer work, for which we need our eyes and our fingers, so we can expect that both will get _____.

4   Experts think that our _____ will get smaller because we won't talk so much.

5   They also say that our little toe will _____.

6   In the future, we'll grow less _____.

2 **Read the text quickly. Which of these inventions produces electricity, and where does the energy come from?**

It's the _____. The energy comes from _____.

3 ✳ **Read the text again. Are sentences 1–5 'Right' (A) or 'Wrong' (B)? If there isn't enough information to answer 'Right' or 'Wrong', choose 'Doesn't say' (C).**

0   If you have the Things Spotter you'll never lose things again.   A   B   Ⓒ

1   The Things Spotter won't be very expensive.   A   B   C

2   The Fire Recharger turns solar energy into flames.   A   B   C

3   The Fire Recharger will be good to have when there is no electricity.   A   B   C

4   DigiGoggles will make scuba diving easier.   A   B   C

5   People will be able to use DigiGoogles for surfing the web.   A   B   C

The future of …

Losing things … and finding them again!

If you are one of those people who often lose things, you'll be happy with an invention that will soon become very popular – or so experts think. The Things Spotter will allow you to find everything, from your wallet to your cat. It'll look like a small key tag that you can put on your wallet or your cat, and it won't cost a lot. The tag will be connected to your mobile phone via BlueTooth technology. When you lose something, you'll press a button on your mobile and a map on your screen will tell you where to look.

Charging your phone in the wilderness

Imagine going camping in the wilderness. You have no electricity, and you need to make an urgent phone call. The batteries on your mobile are empty. Some engineers are working on a Fire Recharger. It turns heat from fire into electricity. This means you will be able to charge your empty batteries if you use a small gas fire, or even a wood campfire. When this gadget is in the shops, it'll be good to have at home too. It'll help people to stay in contact, even if there are power cuts, for example because of heavy storms.

Underwater photography

Don't you love them too – those colourful underwater photos of tropical fish and coral reefs? But these photos are not easy to take. Underwater photography is an expensive hobby, and good equipment is also very, very heavy. But heavy underwater cameras will soon be a thing of the past. Maybe in a few years' time you will buy a pair of DigiGoggles before you go on holiday. That's the name of a special diving mask that can take photos too. And you probably won't even have to press a button to get a good shot. Open and close your eyes twice and your camera will go 'click'!

DEVELOPING WRITING

Taking phone messages

1 ◀)48 **Listen to the conversation. Why can't Neil take the call?** (Circle) **the correct answer.**

A He's having lunch.

B He's out shopping.

C He's in a meeting.

2 ◀)48 **Listen again. Read the secretary's message for Neil. Which two pieces of information in the message are wrong?**

1 _____

2 _____

To: Neil

Tim called. He says he booked a taxi for 7 o'clock tomorrow morning. The driver thinks it'll take two hours to get to the airport. Tim says there's enough time to meet the TV people after the flight. You can reach him on his mobile. I've got a doctor's appointment now. I'll be back shortly after 4. Please text me if anything's not clear.

Best,
Grace

3 Grace wrote another phone message on the same day. Read it. Then answer the questions.

Isaac,

Just got home after busy day. Samuel's mum phoned. Told me Maths test didn't go well. She says no pocket money for Samuel for two weeks. We need to talk, too. Off to gym now. Back 9.30. See you then.

Love (worried),
Mum

1 Which of the two messages is formal?

A the message to Neil   B the message to Isaac

2 Write the names of the people she writes to.

She finishes the message to [1]_____ in a formal way.

She finishes the message to [2]_____ in an informal way.

In the message to [3]_____ she writes full sentences.

In the message to [4]_____ she leaves out certain words.

4 Grace left these words out in her message to Isaac. Where could they go? Rewrite the message in your notebooks.

a | the | I | she | there's
I'm | the | at | I'll be | I'll

Writing tip: taking a phone message

Listen carefully and make notes about the most important information. Write down key words:

- Who phoned?
- Who is the message for?
- What is the message?
- What's the caller's phone number / email?

After the phone call, write out the message. You can leave out words that are not so important in informal messages – but only if the message is still clear:

- personal pronouns: *I, we, he, she*, etc.
- prepositions: *to, at, on, in*, etc.
- auxiliary verbs: *is, am, are*, etc.
- articles: *the, a, an*

5 Read the note. Cross out all the words that can be left out.

Hi Sandy,

Thomas called. He wanted to ask you about the French homework. There are a few things he doesn't understand. Also he wants to go and see a film tonight. Are you interested? Can you please call him back? His new mobile number is 87964 0360.

Leah

6 ◀)49 **Listen to the conversations. Take the messages the callers want to leave.**

- Decide whether the message is formal or informal.
- Make sure you include the most important information.
- When your message is finished, read it again. Ask yourself, 'Will the message be clear to the person who it is for?'

MESSAGE FROM: _____

MESSAGE FOR: _____

MESSAGE: _____

_____

_____

_____

CONTACT DETAILS: _____

LISTENING

1 🔊50 Listen to the conversations. Circle A, B or C.

Conversation 1

How does Jack feel about the Biology project?

A fed up

B excited

C bored

Conversation 2

How does Ryan see the future of food?

A We'll eat pills.

B We won't eat pasta.

C We'll still eat normal food.

Conversation 3

What does Sue think Sofia should do so that she will feel good again?

A go to the gym

B go dancing

C lie in the sun

2 🔊50 Listen to the conversations again and write (T) true or (F) false.

Conversation 1

1 Jack won't enjoy the project. ☐

2 They will have to work hard. ☐

Conversation 2

3 Ryan doesn't like pasta. ☐

4 Ava thinks robots will cook for them. ☐

Conversation 3

5 Sue is on her way to the park. ☐

6 Sofia likes lying in the sun. ☐

DIALOGUE

1 Complete the conversation. Use the correct phrases to express sympathy.

What a shame | sorry to hear | Poor

ALEX   Hi, Naomi. What seems to be the problem?

NAOMI   It's about Chris, my brother.

ALEX   What about him?

NAOMI   He's in hospital.

ALEX   I'm ¹_____ that, Naomi. What happened?

NAOMI   He broke his leg.

ALEX   ²_____ Chris!

NAOMI   Yes. We wanted to go to the concert on Sunday. Now we can't go.

ALEX   ³_____.

2 Complete the short conversation. Use phrases to express sympathy. Use this situation.

Matthew notices that his friend Owen has a problem. He asks him about it and finds out that Owen lost his wallet on the way to the shopping centre. He lost all his money. He wanted to buy a new MP3 player and can't buy one now.

MATTHEW   Hi, Owen. How are you?

OWEN   _____

_____

_____

_____

_____

_____

PHRASES FOR FLUENCY SB p.109

1 Complete the conversation. Replace the phrases in *italics* with phrases from the list.

I suppose so. | I mean | Whatever. | I can't wait. Wait and see. | Tell you what.

ADRIAN   Looks like it'll start raining pretty soon.

SHEILA   ⁰*I think perhaps you are right.*

ADRIAN   ¹*I really don't care.* I've got so much work to do, so I can't go out anyway.

SHEILA   ²*Here's what I think.* I could help you, then we could go out together. ³*What I want to say is*, if that's OK with you, of course.

GAVIN   ⁴*I'm very excited.* If the weather's OK, we'll climb a mountain on Saturday. It's 3,560 metres high!

ANNE   Wow. That's a lot of walking. Do you think you'll be strong enough?

GAVIN   ⁵*We'll know in the future.*

0 *I suppose so.*_____

1 _____

2 _____

3 _____

4 _____

5 _____

Reading and Writing part 8

1 Read the information about a doctor's appointment. Complete Dan's notes.

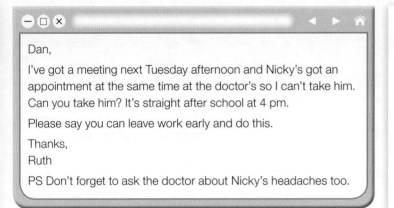

Dan,

I've got a meeting next Tuesday afternoon and Nicky's got an appointment at the same time at the doctor's so I can't take him. Can you take him? It's straight after school at 4 pm.

Please say you can leave work early and do this.

Thanks,
Ruth

PS Don't forget to ask the doctor about Nicky's headaches too.

Garden Lane Medical Centre
14 Garden Lane
Warrington
Phone 01033 325 786

<u>Patient name:</u> <u>Nicholas Holmes</u>

Just to inform you there is a change to your appointment with Dr Glass. The date is now Tuesday 13 October at the same time of 4 pm.

Please let us know if you are unable to make this appointment. Otherwise there is no need to reply. Sorry if this causes you a problem.

Nicky's appointment:

Date: ⁰ _Tuesday 13 October_ Address: ³_____

Time: ¹_____ Phone: ⁴_____

Doctor: ²_____ Don't forget to ask about: ⁵_____

Exam guide: information transfer

In a form completion question, you will read two short texts and use them to complete some notes about the information they contain.

- You need to read <u>both</u> texts carefully before you try to complete the notes.
- Often information in one text will be different from the information in the other one. This is because the second text often talks about changes. You need to make sure you use the most current information to complete the note.

- Sometimes you will need to work out dates and times using clues in the texts. For example, the first text might say *Let's meet at 10 am* and the second might say *I'll be an hour late*. From these clues the answer for 'time of meeting' will be *11 am*.
- If you have time, always check your answers to see if you missed anything.

2 Read the information about a school trip. Complete Seb's notes.

Dear Seb,

I got the tickets – we're going to see MegaMan! I'm coming up the night before. Can I stay the night at your house? My train arrives at 6 pm. Can you meet me at the station?

Can't wait!
Paul

PS You owe me £25 for the show.

Liverpool Apollo Theatre

Thursday 8 May – One Night Only

MegaMan – Live

Doors open at 7 pm

Paul arrives on: ⁰ _Wednesday 7 May_   Name of concert hall: ³_____

Meet him at the station at: ¹_____   Need to get to the theatre by: ⁴_____ o'clock.

Date of show: ²_____   Ticket costs: ⁵ £_____

12 TRAVELLERS' TALES

GRAMMAR
Present perfect simple SB p.112

1 ★★★ **Find twelve past participles in the word search. Use the irregular verb list on page 128 to help you.**

R	D	S	L	E	P	T	S	F
T	O	W	S	L	E	E	P	L
A	N	U	V	U	M	S	O	E
K	E	M	S	E	E	N	K	W
E	B	W	R	I	T	T	E	N
N	O	W	R	O	T	E	N	A
A	U	F	L	O	W	N	G	R
S	G	W	A	N	O	R	O	N
T	H	D	G	O	N	E	E	O
O	T	H	E	R	T	A	S	D

0	buy	_bought_	6	sleep	_____
1	do	_____	7	speak	_____
2	fly	_____	8	swim	_____
3	go	_____	9	take	_____
4	meet	_____	10	win	_____
5	see	_____	11	write	_____

2 ★★★ **Complete the sentences. Use the past participles from Exercise 1.**

0 I have never ___*flown*___ in a plane.

1 My brother has _____ to a lot of football matches this year.

2 I don't want to watch that film – I've _____ it five times!

3 I'm having a great holiday. I've _____ hundreds of photographs!

4 He's really tired because he's _____ fifty emails today.

5 They haven't got any money left because they've _____ so many things.

6 My dad's really happy because he's _____ a competition.

7 The teacher's angry with us because we haven't _____ our homework.

3 ★★★ **When Jenny was 12, she wrote a list of things she wanted to do. Jenny is now 75. Write sentences about what she has and hasn't done. Use the present perfect form of the verbs.**

0	write a book	✓
1	see the Himalaya mountains	✓
2	fly in a hot air balloon	✗
3	meet the president	✗
4	sleep under the stars	✓
5	swim to France	✗
6	win a tennis tournament	✗
7	go for a walk in the snow – with no shoes!	✓

0 *She's written a book.* _____

1 _____

2 _____

3 _____

4 _____

5 _____

6 _____

7 _____

been to vs. gone to SB p.112

4 ★★★ **Match the pictures and the sentences.**

0	He's been to China.	b
1	He's gone to China.	
2	They've been to the supermarket.	
3	They've gone to the supermarket.	

Present perfect with *ever* / *never*

`SB p.113`

5 ★★☆ **Put the words in order to make questions and answers.**

0 A you / ever / a / won / Have / competition
   Have you ever won a competition?

 B never / I've / No, / anything / won
   No, I've never won anything.

1 A been / Has / New York / to / ever / she
   _____

 B never / the USA / she's / to / been / No,
   _____

2 A you / eaten / ever / Have / food / Japanese
   _____

 B restaurant / been / never / No, / Japanese / I've / to / a
   _____

3 A ever / they / in a helicopter / Have / flown
   _____

 B never / flown / they've / in a helicopter or a plane / No,
   _____

4 A your parents / Have / ever / angry with you / been
   _____

 B they've / angry / with me / lots of times / Yes, / been
   _____

Present perfect vs. past simple `SB p.115`

6 ★★☆ **Complete the conversations. Use the present perfect or past simple form of the verbs in brackets.**

1 A Let's go and eat some Indian food.
 B But I 0 *'ve never eaten* (never/eat) Indian food.
 A No, you're wrong! You 1_____ (eat) Indian food at my house last week.
 B Really? Oh yes – you 2_____ (make) a curry! I remember now.

2 A My parents 3_____ (travel) to lots of places round the world.
 B 4_____ (they/visit) China?
 A Oh, yes, they 5_____ (go) to Beijing two years ago. They 6_____ (love) it there.
 B They're lucky. I 7_____ (always/want) to go to China, but I 8_____ (never/have) the chance.

Pronunciation

Sentence stress

Go to page 121.

7 ★★★ **Complete the email. Use the present perfect or past simple form of the verbs in brackets.**

Hi Mark,

Sorry I 0 *haven't written* (write) to you recently – the thing is, I 1_____ (be) really busy in June and July!

Anyway, I've got news for you. Two things 2_____ (happen) that are important for me.

So, my first big news is that last week I 3_____ (go) to a party at my friend's house and I 4_____ (meet) a really nice girl called Joanna. We 5_____ (talk) the whole evening and we 6_____ (get) on together really well.

So that's good, eh? Only there's a problem, because at the end of the evening she 7_____ (ask) me to go ice-skating with her. Of course I 8_____ (say) yes! But I 9_____ (never/try) ice-skating before. Should I go? I don't want to look stupid, you know?

The other big news is – my parents 10_____ (buy) a house! So next month we won't live in this flat any more. I'm a bit sad because I 11_____ (live) here all my life so far, so it's going to be strange to be in another place. But the new house is great – it's got four bedrooms so my brother and I can each have a room. I 12_____ (never/have) my own bedroom before! I hope you can come and stay some time.

OK, I have to go now. Write soon OK?

Best, Andy

GET IT RIGHT!

Present perfect with *ever* / *never*

We use *never* when we want to say 'at no time in (my/your/his, etc.) life' and we use *ever* when we want to say 'at any time in (my/your/his, etc.) life'.

✓ *I've seen 'War Horse'. It's the best film I've ever seen.*

✗ *I've seen 'War Horse'. It's the best film I've never seen.*

Remember, we don't use *not* and *never* together.

Circle the correct adverb.

1 Lindsay was the best friend I've *never* / *ever* had.

2 I've *never* / *ever* been to London, but I hope to next year.

3 I'm nervous about flying because I've *never* / *ever* done it before.

4 I'm wearing my new shoes. They're the best shoes I've *never* / *ever* had.

5 I have *never* / *ever* visited Paris.

VOCABULARY

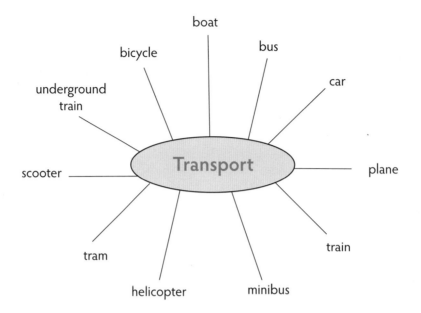

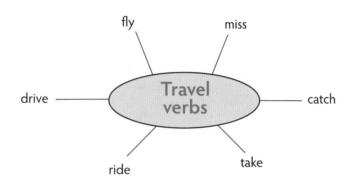

Irregular past participles

been (*go*)   eaten (*eat*)
gone (*go*)   taken (*take*)
done (*do*)   flown (*fly*)
seen (*see*)   swum (*swim*)
written (*write*)   won (*win*)
met (*meet*)   made (*make*)
spoken (*speak*)   driven (*drive*)

Key words in context

continent	The biggest **continent** is Asia.
journey	The **journey** from Japan to France is very long.
neighbour	We have a nice flat but our **neighbours** are terrible – they make a lot of noise!
skeleton	We found some bones on the hill – it was the **skeleton** of a dog.
take a risk	You can't always be safe – sometimes you have to **take a risk**.
tiny	It was a very small mistake – a **tiny** mistake!
tourist	The centre of Paris is always full of **tourists**.
tracks	There was an accident when the train came off the **tracks**.
traveller	Nora Dunn is a professional **traveller**.

Transport and travel SB p.115

1 ★☆☆ **Look at the pictures. Use them to complete the puzzle. What is the 'mystery' word?**

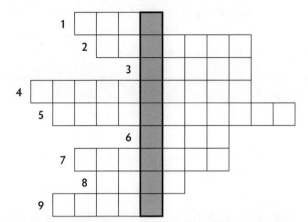

2 ★★☆ **Match the methods of travel and the definitions.**

0 a minibus — *g*
1 (an) underground (train) ☐
2 a tram ☐
3 a boat ☐
4 a plane ☐
5 a bicycle ☐
6 a train ☐
7 a scooter ☐
8 a helicopter ☐

a an electric 'train' in cities, for carrying people
b a small motorbike
c something that travels on tracks and carries people
d something that flies and can fly up, down or stay still
e a train that goes below the ground
f something for travelling on water
g a small bus with seats for about ten people
h something with two wheels that you sit on and move with your legs and feet
i something that flies, with engine(s) and wings

Travel verbs SB p.115

3 ★☆☆ **Complete the sentences. Use the verbs in the list.**

~~flies~~ | drive | catch | misses | rides | take

0 Aziz is a pilot. He __*flies*__ A380 planes for Emirate Airlines.
1 I don't go by car. I always _____ the train.
2 He hasn't got a car because he can't _____ .
3 She is always at the station ten minutes before her train leaves. She never _____ it.
4 Every weekend he takes his motorbike and _____ it all the way to Scotland.
5 Please don't be late! It's really important that we _____ the 10.30 train.

4 ★★☆ **Complete the sentences. Use the correct form of the travel verbs.**

0 Last year we __*flew*__ from London to Los Angeles.
1 Sometimes I'm late for school because I _____ the bus.
2 My mum _____ to work every day – in her twenty-year old car!
3 On Sunday afternoons, when I'm bored, I go out and _____ my bike for an hour or two.
4 Hurry up! We have to _____ the 10 o'clock train!
5 When we got back to the airport, we _____ a taxi home.

READING

1 REMEMBER AND CHECK (Circle) **the correct words. Check your answers in the blog on page 111 of the Student's Book.**

0 Nora Dunn is a professional (*traveller*) / *tourist*.

1 When she was 30, she made a big *mistake* / *decision*.

2 Nora *has* / *hasn't* got rich parents who help her to travel.

3 She has been on TV in *three* / *five* countries.

4 She helped people in Burma and Thailand when *a cyclone* / *an earthquake* hit their countries.

5 Nora writes *in a magazine* / *on a website* to give advice to travellers.

2 Read the story. Answer the questions.

1 What question do the two travellers ask the old man?

_____

2 What two different answers does he give them?

_____

One evening, an old man was sitting on a bench on the top of a hill. He was looking down at the town where he lived, down in the valley below him.

Just then, a traveller walked up to him – a man carrying a stick with a small bag on it containing his possessions. He stopped beside the old man to talk to him.

'Excuse me, sir,' the traveller said. 'I am going to the town down there, the town in the valley. Do you know it?'

'Yes,' said the old man. 'I know it.'

'Well,' said the traveller. 'Can you tell me – what are the people like in that town?'

The old man thought for a bit. Then he said, 'Tell me – what were the people like in the last town you were in?'

3 Answer the questions.

0 What was the old man looking at when he was on the bench?

He was looking at the town where he lived.

1 What did the first traveller say about the people in the last town he was in?

_____

2 What did the first traveller decide to do – go to the town or not?

_____

3 What were the people like in the last town the second traveller was in?

_____

4 Where did the second traveller go when he left the old man?

_____

4 What does the story tell us? Choose one explanation.

1 If we travel to different places, we will meet all kinds of different people and we can visit them.

2 Whether a place and the people there are nice or not is up to us.

3 Before we visit a place, it's a good idea to ask questions about the people who live there.

'Oh,' said the traveller. 'They were awful – horrible people. They didn't like me, and I didn't like them.'

And the old man said, 'I'm sorry to tell you that the people in the town in the valley are horrible too. You won't like them.'

'OK,' said the traveller. And he walked away. He didn't go to the town in the valley.

About an hour later, another traveller arrived near the old man.

'Excuse me, sir,' the second traveller said. 'I am going to the town down there, the town in the valley. Do you know it?'

'Yes,' said the old man. 'I know it.'

'Well,' said the second traveller. 'Can you tell me – what are the people like in that town?'

The old man thought for a bit. Then he said, 'Tell me – what were the people like in the last town you were in?'

'Oh,' said the second traveller. 'They were wonderful – really nice people. They liked me, and I loved them.'

And the old man said, 'I'm happy to tell you that the people in the town in the valley are wonderful too. You are going to like them very much.'

'Oh, thank you!' said the second traveller. And he walked happily down to the town in the valley.

DEVELOPING WRITING

A composition

1 Read the advertisement for a competition in a teenage magazine. Answer the questions.

1 What do you have to write about?

_____

2 How many winners are there?

_____

3 What is the prize for the winners?

_____

HAVE YOU EVER IMAGINED YOUR LIFE IN THE FUTURE? WHEN YOUR DREAMS HAVE COME TRUE?

Write a composition and tell us about you in twenty years' time – where you are and what you've done. (Don't write 'I' – use your name and 'he' or 'she'.)

The winners – there will be three of them! – get a trip to our magazine headquarters in London, to spend a day talking to us and meeting some of the people we write about!

Send your entry to us at:
competition@teenzines.com

CLOSING DATE: 21 DECEMBER

---

2 Read Jackie's entry composition for the competition. Put the paragraphs in order.

3 It's important in a 'biography' like this to show the times when things happened. Read Jackie's composition again. Complete the phrases that she uses.

0 __From__ 2015 __to__ 2021
1 A year _____ ,
2 _____ she left school
3 at _____ 22
4 After _____ years,
5 _____ 2035,

Writing tip: a composition

This writing task asks you to imagine yourself in the future – and in the future you are doing what you dream of doing. Think about these things.

1 How old is the 'future you'?
2 What are you doing? Where do you live?
3 What happened (e.g. at school) that started you on the road to where you are now?
4 Who helped you?
5 Are you famous? Are you happy?

---

4 Write your 'story' in the third person, like Jackie did (about 120–160 words). Remember to use time expressions.

From Bradford to Boston!

[ ] **A** After a couple of years, her boss asked to see her. 'How about working in the USA?' he said. 'Our owners have a newspaper there. They want you to work for them. In Boston!' Jackie thought for about two seconds and said, 'Yes!'

[ ] **B** From 2015 to 2021, Jackie was a student at the Bridges High School in Bradford. She did well at school and enjoyed writing. But her great love was always films – she went to the cinema, she read film magazines, she watched older films on the Internet. Her dream was to work in the USA.

[ ] **C** So now, in 2035, she lives and works in Boston. She's been to film festivals all over the world and she's met almost all the great film stars of the 2020s. Her dream has come true!

[1] **D** Jackie Stephenson, from Bradford, England, is the film critic for an American magazine. Here's her story.

[ ] **E** So, when her school started an online magazine, it was clear that she was going to write about films! A year later, the local newspaper heard about her and when she left school, they invited her to do a weekly film column.

[ ] **F** Jackie enjoyed working for the local newspaper but soon she wanted to do more. So, she started her own film website at the age of 22. But she went on writing for the newspaper too.

LISTENING

1 🔊52 **Listen to the conversations, A and B. Match the topics with the conversations.**

0	jobs	B
1	being a waiter	☐
2	the important things in your life	☐
3	a house	☐
4	restaurants	☐

2 🔊52 **Listen again. Complete the sentences.**

A Gary and Martha

Martha has [0] *always lived* in this house.

Her parents moved from their flat when she
[1] _____ .

Everything important in Martha's life
[2] _____ in this house.

B Sue and Uncle Paul

Uncle Paul works in a [3] _____ .

He has also been a [4] _____ and a
[5] _____ .

He hated being a [6] _____ but he loved
being a [7] _____ .

He has [8] _____ a job.

DIALOGUE

1 🔊52 **Put the conversations in order. Then listen again to check.**

Conversation A

1	GARY	This is a nice house, Martha. Have you always lived here?
☐	GARY	Like what, for example?
☐	GARY	Where have they lived, then?
☐	GARY	Because it's big?
☐	GARY	Oh right. And when you were born, they moved?
☐	MARTHA	Well, a long time ago, they lived in a small flat. Before I was born.
☐	MARTHA	Oh, Gary, I'm not going to tell you!
☐	MARTHA	Yes, we have. Well, I've always lived here, but of course my parents have lived in other places.
☐	MARTHA	Yes, they needed more room. Anyway, I've always loved this house.
☐	MARTHA	No, I don't think it's very big. It's because everything important in my life has happened here.

Conversation B

1	SUE	Uncle Paul? You work in a bank, right?
☐	SUE	A waiter? Really?
☐	SUE	Oh right. And you've been a taxi driver too?
☐	SUE	Have you ever not had a job?
☐	SUE	What other jobs?
☐	SUE	But have you always worked in a bank?
☐	PAUL	No, not always. I've done other jobs too.
☐	PAUL	Yes, that's right.
☐	PAUL	Well, let me think. I've been a waiter and I've been a taxi driver.
☐	PAUL	Yes, I was a waiter when I was at university. Just weekends and holidays. Hard work but good fun! I loved it.
☐	PAUL	No, I've always had a job. I've been very lucky.
☐	PAUL	Yes, I drove a taxi for almost a year. I hated it!

▰▰▰ TRAIN TO THiNK ▰▰▰

Exploring differences

1 **Look at the phrases about jobs in the left-hand column. Are they true about only waiters, about only taxi drivers, or about both? Tick (✓) the correct column.**

You …	waiters	taxi drivers	both
meet a lot of people.			✓
spend a long time on your feet.			
have to carry things.			
can work in any weather.			
have to remember things.			
wear special clothes.			

2 **Think about houses and flats. What things are the same? What things are different? Write three more things in the left-hand column. Tick (✓) the correct column.**

It …	house	flat	both
has got bedrooms.			✓
_____			
_____			
_____			

CAMBRIDGE ENGLISH: Key

Reading and Writing part 9

1 **Read Georgina's email. Imagine you are Jana. Write an email to Georgina and answer her questions (about 25–35 words).**

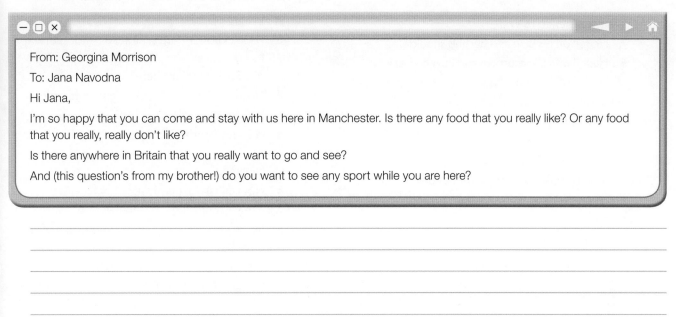

From: Georgina Morrison

To: Jana Navodna

Hi Jana,

I'm so happy that you can come and stay with us here in Manchester. Is there any food that you really like? Or any food that you really, really don't like?

Is there anywhere in Britain that you really want to go and see?

And (this question's from my brother!) do you want to see any sport while you are here?

Exam guide: guided writing

This exam exercise tests your ability to write a short email / letter / post. You need to:

- Make sure that you do what the task asks you – in other words, write an email (starting, for example, *Hi Georgina*) and answer all three of the questions (in this example, they are about food, places to visit and sport).

- Write the number of words you are asked to write (not fewer than 25, not more than 35).
- Make your English grammar and vocabulary as good as it can be – but the most important thing is to be clear, and to do the points explained above!

2 **Read Alex's email. Imagine you are Rodrigo. Write an email to Alex and answer his questions (about 25–35 words).**

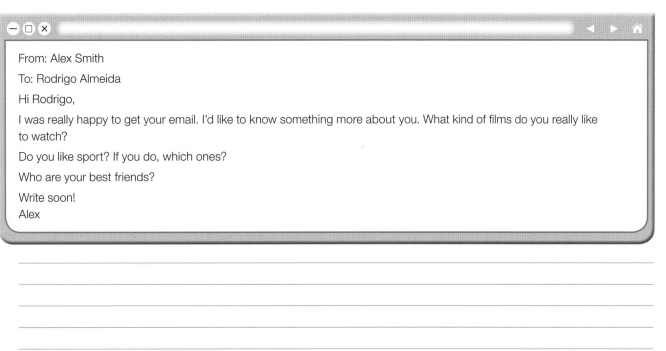

From: Alex Smith

To: Rodrigo Almeida

Hi Rodrigo,

I was really happy to get your email. I'd like to know something more about you. What kind of films do you really like to watch?

Do you like sport? If you do, which ones?

Who are your best friends?

Write soon!

Alex

CONSOLIDATION

LISTENING

1 🔊 **53** **Listen to the conversation. Circle A, B or C.**

1 What happened to Will?
   A He fell off his bike and hurt his shoulder.
   B He fell off his motorbike and hurt his back.
   C He fell off his motorbike and hurt his shoulder.

2 What does Will think is dangerous?
   A driving in traffic
   B riding a bicycle
   C riding a motorbike

3 How does Will usually get to work now?
   A by motorbike
   B by car
   C by bus

2 🔊 **53** **Listen again. Answer the questions.**

0 When did Will buy his motorbike?
   He bought it two weeks ago.

1 Why did he buy a motorbike?
   _____

2 Why doesn't he want to use the underground?
   _____

3 When will Will get on his motorbike again?
   _____

4 What does he like about going to work by bus?
   _____

3 **Complete the sentences with *been* or *gone*.**

TIM   Your dad travels a lot. Where is he this time?
ALICE He's ¹_____ to Brazil.
TIM   Lucky him! Have you ever ²_____ to Brazil?
ALICE No, I haven't. I've never ³_____ anywhere outside Europe.
TIM   Where's your sister by the way?
ALICE She's ⁴_____ to the dentist's with my mum.
TIM   I haven't ⁵_____ to the dentist's for a long time.

GRAMMAR

4 **Complete the conversations. Use the present perfect form of the verbs in brackets.**

0 A Where's Jack?
   B I don't know. I _*haven't seen*_ (not see) him today.

1 A Are Steve and Julie here?
   B No, they _____ (go) to the cinema.

2 A Is there any food in the kitchen?
   B No – my brother _____ (eat) it all!

3 A _____ (you/write) to your Aunt Paula?
   B Not yet. I'll do it tonight.

4 A Are you enjoying Los Angeles?
   B It's great. I _____ (meet) lots of nice people.

5 A Have you got a lot of homework?
   B No, only a little – and I _____ (do) it all!

6 A Is this a good book?
   B I don't know. I _____ (not read) it.

7 A Why are you so happy?
   B My parents _____ (give) me a new bike for my birthday!

VOCABULARY

5 **Complete the words.**

0 Can we watch this film? I haven't s *e e n* it before, but everyone says it's great.

1 Some really rich people fly between cities by h _ _ _ _ _ _ _ _ _.

2 He can't walk now because he's broken his a _ _ _ _.

3 In some European cities you can still see t _ _ _ s that run on metal tracks.

4 He looked really bored, with his e _ _ _ _ s on the table and his head between his hands.

5 Wow! It's my first time on a plane! I've never f _ _ _ _ before today!

6 We were late, so we didn't c _ _ _ _ the train.

7 The dog was really hot – its t _ _ _ _ _ was hanging out of its mouth.

6 Circle the correct words.

JAKE Hi, Mum. I've ⁰*been* / *gone* into town – and look! I've ¹*buy* / *bought* a new shirt.

MUM It's nice, Jake. But isn't it a bit small? You're tall and you've got big ²*shoulders* / *ankles*.

JAKE No, Mum, it's fine. I think ³*I wear* / *I'll wear* it to Andrea's party on Saturday.

MUM Oh, is she having a party?

JAKE Yes, it's for her birthday. ⁴*She's invited* / *She invites* everyone from school.

MUM But her birthday ⁵*was* / *has been* last month!

JAKE I know. But her mother was ill, so she couldn't have a party until now.

MUM Oh, I'm sorry to ⁶*know* / *hear* that. Is her mother OK now?

JAKE Oh, yes, she's ⁷*being* / *doing* OK. She had a problem with her ⁸*stomach* / *knee* – the doctors think she ⁹*ate* / *has eaten* something bad.

MUM Oh, ¹⁰*sorry* / *poor* her. Well, please tell Andrea that I hope the party is great.

JAKE Thanks, Mum. I'll tell her when I ¹¹*see* / *will see* her.

DIALOGUE

7 Complete the conversation. Use the words in the list. There are two that you don't need.

~~been~~ | as soon as | doing | gone | hear | if
knee | poor | shame | went | will | won't

PAUL Hi, Jacky. Where have you ⁰____*been*____ ?

JACKY At the doctor's. I have a pain in my ¹_____ .

PAUL Oh, I'm sorry to ²_____ that. Is everything OK now?

JACKY So-so. I'll have to see him again ³_____ it doesn't get better.

PAUL ⁴_____ you.

JACKY Oh, it's not so bad. It hurts a bit but I'm ⁵_____ OK. Listen, I'm looking for Mike. Do you know where he is?

PAUL Oh, he isn't here. He's ⁶_____ to see his grandmother. She's ill. He ⁷_____ be back until about six o'clock.

JACKY That's a ⁸_____ . I really want to talk to him. Can you ask him to call me, please?

PAUL Sure. I'll ask him ⁹_____ he gets back.

READING

8 Read the text about children and schools in Niger. Answer the questions.

0 In Niger, what percentage of people have running water at home?

20% of people have running water at home.

1 Who often goes to get water for a family?

_____

2 Why is Sani often two hours late for school?

_____

3 Why does Badjeba sometimes fall asleep in lessons?

_____

4 Why do families send children to get water when it makes them late for school?

_____

SCHOOL OR WATER?

Niger, in central Africa, is a country that has very little rain. And 80% of people have no running water at home. So water is very important in people's lives, but sometimes it means that kids don't do well at school.

Children are often the ones who have to find water for the family. They go out on donkeys and travel up to ten kilometres to get water. And then they are late for school, or they don't go at all. Sani, 11, gets water for his family in the morning and usually gets to school at 10 o'clock – two hours late. 'Some of the other children are lucky,' he says. 'They don't have to get water. And so they learn more quickly than me.'

It's hard for the children to study. One girl, Badjeba, says, 'I get up at 4.30 to get water, five kilometres away. Then I take it home. Then I walk to school. I'm exhausted. I'm so tired that I fall asleep in the lessons. And after school, I have to go and find water again.'

In one classroom, the teacher asks: 'How many of you were late today because you had to get water?' And about 90% of the kids put their hand up. Their families send them to get water – school is important, but water is life.

WRITING

9 Imagine you are either Sani or Badjeba (or one of the children in the Culture text on page 116 of the Student's Book). Write a diary entry for a school day (about 100–120 words). Write about these things.

- Getting to school.
- What you did at school.
- Going home.

PRONUNCIATION

UNIT 1
Plurals and third person verb endings: /s/, /z/ or /ɪz/

1 Add *-s* or *-es* to the present simple verbs. Write them in the correct column.

~~cook~~ | dance | enjoy | finish
give | need | play | relax | sleep | swim
take | want | wash | watch | write

/s/ – works	/z/ – lives	/ɪz/ – closes
cooks		

2 🔊04 Listen, check and repeat.

3 Complete the sentences with the plural nouns.

~~blogs~~ | bikes | buses | cats | players
puzzles | stamps | quizzes

0 Jane enjoys writing cooking and sport ___*blogs*___ . /z/

1 Julie's favourite games are crosswords and _____ . /z/

2 Luke's got lots of pets – a dog, some fish and four black and white _____ . /s/

3 The girls in that team are all good _____ . /z/

4 Julie watches _____ on TV. /ɪz/

5 Many students like riding their _____ in the park. /s/

6 Jenny catches the red _____ in London. /ɪz/

7 Lewis collects _____ and bottle tops. /s/

4 🔊05 Listen, check and repeat.

UNIT 2
Contractions

1 Match the rhyming words.

0 I'm   a here
1 she's   b time
2 they're   c chair
3 it's   d please
4 we're   e sits

2 🔊07 Listen, check and repeat.

3 Now match these rhyming words.

0 who's   f door
5 we've   g years
6 let's   h choose
7 you're   i gets
8 here's   j leave

4 🔊08 Listen, check and repeat.

UNIT 3
Vowel sounds: /ɪ/ and /iː/

1 🔊14 Put your finger on *Start*. Listen to the words. Go left if you hear the /ɪ/ sound and right if you hear the /iː/ sound. Say the name. You'll hear the words twice.

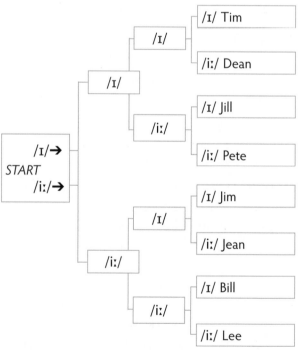

0 milk – cheese – peas. Who do you meet? ___*Pete*___

1 _____ 2 _____ 3 _____ 4 _____ 5 _____

2 🔊15 Listen, check and repeat.

UNIT 4
er /ə/ at the end of words

1 Complete the sentences with the words in the list.

later | after | answer | daughter
father | other | paper | writer

0 Ten minutes ____later____ an ambulance was there.

1 My friend Sara wants to be a _____.

2 I don't know the _____ to that question.

3 Our teacher always asks us to speak to each _____ in English.

4 Please write your answers on a separate piece of _____.

5 That little girl over there is Mr Power's _____.

6 My _____'s a farmer. He works very hard.

7 Can you come to my house _____ school?

2 🔊16 Listen, check and repeat.

UNIT 5
Regular past tense endings

1 How many syllables are there? Write them in the columns.

asked | closed | rested | missed | needed
played | shouted | started | tried | wanted

one syllable /d/ or /t/	two syllables /ɪd/
asked	rested

2 🔊21 Listen, check and repeat.

3 (Circle) the correct words to complete the rule.
The -ed endings of regular verbs in the past simple are [1]*pronounced as a separate syllable / not pronounced as a separate syllable*, /ɪd/ when the infinitive form of the verb ends in /t/ or /d/ only.

In all other cases, the -ed endings are [2]*pronounced as a separate syllable / not pronounced as a separate syllable*, but as /t/ or /d/.

4 Write the words ending in the /t/ and /d/ sounds in the correct column.

carried | cooked | enjoyed | finished | helped
loved | stayed | tried | worked | washed

/t/ – ask**ed**	/d/ – clos**ed**
cooked	carried

5 🔊22 Listen, check and repeat.

UNIT 6
Stressed syllables in words

1 Write the words in the correct columns.

adventurous | confident | friendly | interesting
good | helpful | intelligent | nice

1	One syllable	2	Two syllables
	_____		_____
	_____		_____
3	**Three syllables**	**4**	**Four syllables**
	_____		____adventurous____
	_____		_____

2 🔊24 Listen, check and repeat.

3 Which syllable is stressed? Write the words in the correct columns.

confident | adventurous | interesting | important
relaxing | disappointed | intelligent | easy-going

1 Ooo	2 oOo	3 oOoo	4 ooOo
confident	_____	_____	_____
_____	_____	_____	_____

4 🔊25 Listen, check and repeat.

UNIT 7
Vowel sounds: /ʊ/ and /uː/

1 🔊32 **What are you buying? Put your finger on *Start*. Listen to the words. Go left if you hear the /ʊ/ sound and right if you hear the /uː/ sound. Say the word at the end. You'll hear the words twice.**

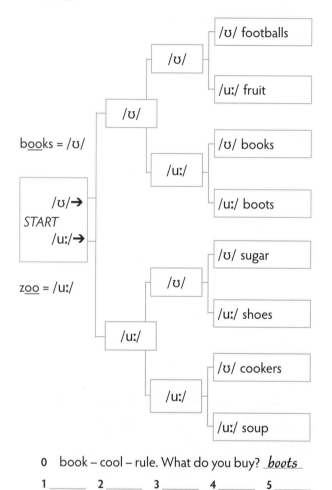

books = /ʊ/

/ʊ/→
START
/uː/→

zoo = /uː/

/ʊ/ footballs
/ʊ/
/uː/ fruit
/ʊ/
/ʊ/ books
/uː/
/uː/ boots

/ʊ/ sugar
/ʊ/
/uː/ shoes
/uː/
/ʊ/ cookers
/uː/
/uː/ soup

    0   book – cool – rule. What do you buy? *boots*

    1 _____   2 _____   3 _____   4 _____   5 _____

2 🔊33 **Listen, check and repeat.**

3 **All of these words are written with the letters 'oo' but they are not pronounced in the same way. Write each word in the /ʊ/ or /uː/ column.**

l̶o̶o̶k̶ | choose | cook | cool
food | good | school | stood

/ʊ/ – foot	/uː/ – room
look	

4 a **Which words rhyme with *should*?**

    _____ and _____.

   b **Which word rhymes with *shoes*?** _____.

5 🔊34 **Listen, check and repeat.**

UNIT 8
Strong and weak forms of *was* and *were*

1 **Write *was*, *wasn't*, *were* or *weren't* to complete the sentences.**

  1 **A** _Was_ she happy to get her new bike?
     B Yes, she _____. She loves it.
  2 **A** _____ they playing volleyball in the park?
     B No, they _____. They _____ at the beach.
  3 **A** Look – that girl _____ at the pool yesterday.
     B No, she _____!
     A Yes, she _____! She's a good swimmer.
     B She _____. The girl we saw had long brown hair.
  4 **A** They _____ very happy with the restaurant last night.
     B Really? Why not?
     A Because they _____ waiting for their food for a long time.
  5 **A** _____ you at the football match last night?
     B No, I _____. I _____ studying for an exam.
     A _____ you? So was I!

2 🔊35 **Listen, check and repeat.**

3 Circle **the stressed forms of these verbs.**

4 🔊35 **Listen again and check.**

UNIT 9
Vowel sounds: /ɪ/ and /aɪ/

1 **Write the words in the columns.**

g̶i̶v̶e̶ | find | fine | gym | list | nice | night
sing | smile | spring | style | thin | wild | wish

/ɪ/ – think	/aɪ/ – drive
give	

2 🔊40 **Listen, check and repeat.**

3 **Match to make sentences.**

  0   I'm going to keep fit   **a** driving at night.
  1   Kim doesn't like   **b** has a healthy lifestyle.
  2   Lions and tigers   **c** ride our bikes.
  3   Mike exercises and   **d** classes at the gym.
  4   It's a nice day so let's   **e** are happier in the wild.

4 🔊41 **Listen and check.**

5 Circle **all of the words in the sentences with the /aɪ/ sound.**

6 🔊42 **Listen, check and repeat.**

UNIT 10
Voiced /ð/ and unvoiced /θ/ consonants

1 **Complete the sentences.**

~~things~~ | clothes | Earth | Maths | months
then | think | third | Thursday | youth

0 There are so many ___*things*___ to do in Sydney.

1 Let's go shopping. I want to buy some new
_____.

2 These three students came first, second and
_____ in the race.

3 My father's birthday's on _____.

4 We had dinner and _____ we went to the
theatre.

5 I _____ we should go out to a restaurant
tonight.

6 We must look after the _____; it's a
beautiful planet.

7 There are twelve _____ in a year.

8 We've got a _____ class after the break.

9 A _____ is a young person.

2 🔊 45 **Listen, check and repeat.**

3 (Circle) all the words in the sentences with a
voiced th sound. <u>Underline</u> all the words with an
unvoiced *th* sound.

UNIT 11
The /h/ consonant sound

1 **Complete the sentences with the words in
the list.**

~~homework~~ | hair | happy | healthy | hear
help | here | hospital | humans | hurt

0 I'll come to your house when I've finished my
History ___*homework*___.

1 It's not _____ to eat too many hamburgers.

2 Harry had to go to the _____ in an
ambulance.

3 That suitcase looks heavy. Can I _____ you
carry it?

4 Helen's got beautiful long black _____.

5 I couldn't _____ the music because the
headphones weren't working.

6 I hope you'll be _____ in your new home.

7 In the future _____ won't have as much hair
as they do now.

8 Hilary _____ her knee while she was
running yesterday.

9 Can you come _____ and help me please?

2 🔊 47 **Listen, check and repeat.**

UNIT 12
Sentence stress

1 **Complete the sentences.**

~~scarf~~ | eggs | English | laptop
farmer | island | cooker | taxi

0 I'm wearing a <u>shirt</u>, a <u>skirt</u>, a <u>hat</u> and a ___*scarf*___.

1 An artist, a doctor, a teacher and a _____.

2 We've got Maths, then Art, then History and then
_____.

3 We need a desk, a lamp, a sofa and a
_____.

4 We caught a plane and then a train and then a bus
and then a _____.

5 We put in flour and sugar and then butter and
_____.

6 For sale: a digital camera, a pen drive, a
microphone and a _____.

7 We saw a lake, a river a jungle and an
_____.

2 🔊 51 **Listen, check and repeat.**

3 **Underline the stressed words in the lists.**

4 🔊 51 **Listen again, check and repeat.**

5 **Look at the stressed words in the sentences
0-7. Then read and (circle) the correct word to
complete the rule.**

We generally stress words like [1]*nouns / articles* that
give us information. We don't generally stress words
like [2]*nouns / articles*.

GRAMMAR REFERENCE

UNIT 1
Present simple

1   We use the present simple for actions that happen repeatedly or habitually.

   *Paul often **goes** to the cinema.*
   *We **have** dinner at 8.00 every evening.*

   We also use the present simple for things that are always or normally true.

   *The sun **comes up** in the east.*
   *We **go** to a big school in London.*

2   With most subjects, the present simple is the same as the base form of the verb. However, with a third person singular subject (*he, she, it*), the verb has an -*s* ending.

   *I **play** tennis on Saturdays.*
   *She **plays** tennis on Saturdays.*

   If a verb ends with -*sh*, -*ch*, -*ss* or -*x*, we add -*es*.

   *he watch**es**, she catch**es**, he miss**es**, she fix**es***

   If a verb ends with consonant + -*y*, we change the -*y* to -*i* and add -*es*.

   *she stud**ies**, he worr**ies***

   If a verb ends with vowel + -*y*, then it is regular.

   play – plays, say – says, buy – buys

3   The negative of the present simple is formed with *don't* (*do not*) or *doesn't* (*does not*) + base form of the verb.

   *I **don't like** carrots.   She **doesn't like** carrots.*

4   Present simple questions and short answers are formed with *do* or *does*.

   ***Do** you **like** cats?   Yes, I **do**. / No, I **don't**.*
   ***Does** Jo **live** here?   Yes, she **does**. / No, she **doesn't**.*

like + -ing

1   After verbs which express likes and dislikes we often use verb + -*ing*.

   *We **love watching** films at home.*
   *My sister **enjoys reading** travel books.*

2   If a verb ends in -*e*, we drop the -*e* before adding -*ing*.

   *live → liv**ing**   ride → rid**ing***

   If a short verb ends in consonant + vowel + consonant, we double the final consonant before adding -*ing*.

   *get → ge**tt**ing, shop → sho**pp**ing, travel → trave**ll**ing*

UNIT 2
Present continuous

1   We use the present continuous for actions that are happening now or around the time of speaking.

   *My friends and I **are playing** an online game at the moment.*
   *It's **raining** now.*

2   The present continuous is formed with the present simple of *be* + verb + -*ing*.

   *I'm **listening to** music.   I'm **not listening** to music.*
   *You're **walking** very fast!   You **aren't walking** very fast.*
   *Alison **is talking** to Jo.   Alison **isn't talking** to Jo.*

3   The question is formed with the present simple of *be* + subject + verb + -*ing*. Short answers are formed using *Yes/No* + pronoun + the correct form of *be* (positive or negative).

   ***Is** Susanna **eating**?   Yes, she **is**. / No, she **isn't**.*
   ***Are** the boys **having** fun?   Yes, they **are**. / No, they **aren't**.*
   *What **are** you **doing**?   Why is she **crying**?*

Verbs of perception

Verbs of perception (*taste / smell / look / sound*) are not used in the present continuous when they are used to give an opinion. They are used in the present simple only.

*This hamburger **doesn't taste** very nice.*

*Mmm! The food **smells** fantastic!*

*These trousers **don't look** very good on me.*

*I don't know who the singer is, but she **sounds** wonderful.*

Present simple vs. present continuous

1   We use different time expressions with the present simple and the present continuous.

   Present simple: *every day, on Mondays, at the weekend, usually, sometimes, often, never*

   Present continuous: *today, right now, at the moment*

   *James **usually walks** to school but **today** he's **taking** the bus.*

2   Some verbs aren't normally used in the continuous form. They are called *state verbs* or *stative verbs* because they talk about a state, not an action. Here are some common examples:

   believe, know, understand, remember, want, need, mean, like, hate
   *I **believe** you. He **knows** a lot about music.*
   *Morgan **wants** to have dinner now.*

UNIT 3
Countable and uncountable nouns

1   Nouns in English are **countable** or **uncountable**.

Countable nouns have both singular and plural forms, for example:

bicycle → bicycles, school → schools, egg → eggs, question → questions, man → men, woman → women, child → children, person → people

But uncountable nouns do not have a plural form. They are always singular, for example:

food, music, money, rice, bread, information

2   **Countable nouns** can take singular or plural verbs.

That car is Japanese.   Those cars are Japanese.
That woman works with me.   Those women work with my mum.

Uncountable nouns always take singular verbs.

This food is horrible.   The music is too loud!

a / an; some / any

1   With singular countable nouns, we can use *a / an* to talk about a specific thing or person.

They've got a car.   She's eating an orange.

2   With plural countable nouns, we use *some* (positive) or *any* (negative).

I want to buy some apples.   We haven't got any eggs.

3   With uncountable nouns, we don't use *a / an* – we use *some / any*, like plural countable nouns.

Let's listen to some music.
I don't want any food.

4   We use *some* to talk about an unspecified number or amount. We normally use *some* in positive sentences.

He bought some fruit in town.

We often use *some* in requests and offers.

Can I have some orange juice, please?
Do you want some cheese?

5   We use *any* to talk about an unspecified number or amount. We normally use *any* in negative sentences, and in questions.

He didn't buy any fruit.
Is there any fruit in the kitchen?

(How) much and (how) many; a lot of / lots of

1   We use *many* with plural countable nouns and *much* with uncountable nouns.

Countable	Uncountable
She doesn't eat many vegetables.	*He doesn't eat much fruit.*
How many children have they got?	*How much time have we got?*

2   We usually use *many* and *much* in negative sentences and questions.

I don't go to many concerts.
How many eggs do you want?

In positive sentences, we normally use *a lot of* or *lots of*. *A lot of / Lots of* can be used with plural countable nouns and with uncountable nouns.

Chris has got lots of / a lot of DVDs.
You can get lots of / a lot of information on the Internet.

too much / too many / not enough + noun

1   If we want to say that the number or amount of something is more than we like or want, we can use *too many* or *too much*. We use *too many* with plural countable nouns, and *too much* with uncountable nouns.

There are too many chairs in the room.
There's too much salt in my food.

2   We use *not enough* with plural countable nouns and with uncountable nouns to say that we think more is / are needed.

There aren't enough chairs in the room.
There isn't enough salt in my food.

too + adjective / (not) + adjective + enough

1   We use *too* + adjective to say that it's more than we like or want.

This soup is too hot.   The clothes are too expensive.

2   We use (*not*) + adjective + *enough* to say that something is less than we like or want.

This bag isn't big enough to put everything in.

UNIT 4
Possessive adjectives

1   Here is the list of possessive adjectives:

Subject pronoun: *I, you, he, she, it, we, they*
Possessive adjectives: *my, your, his, her, its, our, their*

2   We use possessive adjectives to say who something belongs to.

My name's Jack.   Is he your brother?   Look at his hair!   Her bike is really expensive.
The DVD isn't in its box.   They love their cat.

Possessive pronouns

1   Here is the list of possessive pronouns:

Possessive adjective: *my, your, his, her, our, their*
Possessive pronoun: *mine, yours, his, hers, ours, theirs*

2   Possessive pronouns can take the place of possessive adjective + noun.

Is this your book / yours? No, it isn't my book / mine.
I like her hair, but I don't like his.

Whose

When we want to ask a question about who is the owner of something, we use the word *whose*. There are two possible constructions after *whose*.

Whose book is this? or *Whose is this book?*

Possessive *'s*

To talk about possession we can add *'s* to the end of a name / noun.

Annie's bike is really fantastic.
That's my brother's bedroom.

If the name / noun ends in an -*s*, (for example, plural nouns), we add the apostrophe (') after the final -*s*.

That's our neighbours' dog.
I don't like James' shirt.

Past simple of *be* (*was / were*)

1   We use the past simple to talk about actions and events in the past.

2   The past simple of *be* is *was / wasn't* or *were / weren't*.

   I was at school yesterday.   You were late yesterday.
   My sister wasn't there.
   The DVDs weren't very good.

3   Questions with *was / were* are formed by putting the verb before the subject.

   Were you at school yesterday?   Was Maria with you?

UNIT 5
Past simple: regular verbs (positive and negative)

1   In the past simple, regular verbs have an -*ed* ending. The form is the same for all subjects.

   I walked to the park.   You played well yesterday.
   Carla opened the window.

   If a verb ends in -*e*, we add only -*d*.

   like → liked   hate → hated   use → used

   If a verb ends with consonant + -*y*, we change the -*y* to -*i* and add -*ed*.

   study → studied   try → tried   marry → married

   If a short verb ends in consonant + vowel + consonant, we double the final consonant before adding -*ed*.

   stop → stopped   plan → planned   travel → travelled

   If a short verb ends in consonant + vowel + -*y*, it is regular.

   play → played   stay → stayed

2   The past simple negative is formed with *didn't* (*did not*) + base form of the verb. The form is the same for all subjects:

   I / We / She didn't enjoy the film last night.

3   Past time expressions are often used with the past simple.

   Yesterday, yesterday morning, last night, last week, a month ago, two years ago, on Sunday

Modifiers: *very, really, quite*

We use the words *very, really, quite* to say more about an adjective. The words *very* and *really* make an adjective stronger.

The food was good – The food was very good.
The film was exciting – The film was really exciting.

We often use *quite* to say 'a little bit'.

The room was quite small. (= not very small, but a bit small)
The film was quite long. (= not very long, but a bit long)

UNIT 6
Past simple: irregular verbs

A lot of common verbs are irregular. This means that the past simple form is different – they don't have the usual -*ed* ending.

go → went, see → saw, eat → ate, think → thought

The form of the past simple for these verbs is the same for all persons (*I / you / he / she / it / we / they*).

See page 128 for a list of irregular verbs.

The negative of irregular verbs is formed in the same way as regular verbs: *didn't* (*did not*) + base form of the verb.

We didn't enjoy the concert.
I didn't know the answer to the question.

Past simple: (regular and irregular verbs) questions and short answers

1   Past simple questions and short answers are formed with *did*. The form is the same for regular and irregular verbs.

   Did you talk to Barbara this morning?
   Did you see that great match last night?

2   Short answers are formed with *Yes / No* + pronoun + *did / didn't*.

   Did you like the film? Yes, I did.
   Did she phone you last night? No, she didn't.

Double genitive

We use the double genitive to talk about one of many things that we have. We form it with noun + *of* + possessive pronoun (see Unit 4 above). We can also use noun + *of* + noun with possessive *'s*.

He's a friend of mine. (I have many friends)
They are neighbours of ours. (we have many neighbours).

UNIT 7
should / shouldn't

1 When we want to say that something is a good idea (or is a bad idea), we can use *should* or *shouldn't*.

   *I **should study** this weekend.* (I think it's a good idea.)
   *They **shouldn't buy** that car.* (I think it's a bad idea.)
   ***Should** we **go** out tonight?* (Do you think this is a good idea?)

2 *Should* is a modal verb. We use *should / shouldn't* + base form of the verb, and the form is the same for all subjects. We don't use any form of *do* in the negative.

   *I **should try** to study more.*
   *I **shouldn't watch** TV tonight.*
   *You **should listen to** different music.*
   *You **shouldn't listen to** the same things all the time.*

3 Questions are formed with *should* + subject + base form of the verb. Again, we don't use any form of *do* in questions or short answers.

   ***Should** we **tell** her?*
   *Yes, we **should**. / No, we **shouldn't**.*
   ***Should** I **ask** the teacher?*
   *Yes, you **should**. / No, you **shouldn't**.*

have to / don't have to

1 We use *have to* to say that it is necessary or very important to do something.

   *I'm late, I **have to go** now. We **have to be** at school at 8.30.*

   With a third person singular subject (*he, she, it*), we use *has to*.

   *Maggie is very ill – she **has to stay** in bed.*
   *My dad **has to go to** York tomorrow for a meeting.*

2 We use the negative form *don't / doesn't have to* to say that it isn't necessary or important to do something.

   *It's Sunday, so I **don't have to get up early**.*
   *She isn't late – she **doesn't have to hurry**.*

3 We form questions with *do* or *does*.

   ***Do** I **have to go** to the dentist?*
   ***Does** he **have to go** home now?*

4 All forms of *have to* are followed by the base form of the verb.

mustn't vs. don't have to

1 We use *mustn't* to say that it is necessary or very important <u>not</u> to do something.

   *You **mustn't be** late.   I **mustn't forget** to phone Jenny.*

2 *Mustn't* has a different meaning from *don't / doesn't have to*.

   *You **don't have to tell** your friends.* (= It isn't necessary for you to tell them, but you can if you want to.)
   *You **mustn't tell** your friends.* (= Don't tell your friends – it's a secret!)

UNIT 8
Past continuous

1 We use the past continuous to talk about actions in progress at a certain time in the past.

   *In 2012, we **were living** in the USA.*
   *At 4 o'clock yesterday afternoon, I **was sitting** in a Maths lesson.*
   *Last night, the TV was on, but I **wasn't watching** it.*

2 The past continuous is formed with the past simple of *be* + verb + *-ing*.

   *I **was reading** a book. I **wasn't enjoying** it.*
   *You **were running** very fast! But you **weren't winning**!*
   *Jo **was playing** computer games. She **wasn't studying**.*

3 The question is formed with the past simple of *be* + subject + verb + *-ing*. Short answers are formed with *Yes / No* + pronoun + *was / were* or *wasn't / weren't*.

   ***Was** James **running**? Yes, he **was**. / No, he **wasn't**.*
   ***Were** your parents **having** lunch?*
   *Yes, they **were**. / No, they **weren't**.*
   *What **were** you **studying**?   Why **was** she **crying**?*

Past continuous vs. past simple

1 When we talk about the past, we use the past simple for actions that happened at one particular time. We use the past continuous for background actions.

   *When Alex **arrived**, I **was having** dinner.*
   *He **was running** very fast and he **didn't see** the tree.*
   *Sorry, what **did** you **say**? I **wasn't listening**.*

2 We often use *when* with the past simple, and *while* with the past continuous.

   *I was reading **when** the phone **rang**.*
   ***When** my parents **arrived**, we were having a party.*
   *I went into the classroom **while** the teacher **was talking**.*
   ***While** my father **was running**, he fell into a river.*

UNIT 9
Comparative adjectives

1 When we want to compare two things, or two groups of things, we use a comparative form + *than*.

   *I'm **older than** my brother.*
   *France is **bigger than** Britain.*
   *Your computer is **better than** mine.*

2 With short adjectives, we normally add *-er*.

   old → older   cheap → cheaper   clever → cleverer

   If the adjective ends in *-e*, we only add *-r*.

   nice → nicer   safe → safer

   If the adjective ends with consonant + *-y*, we change the *-y* to *-i* and add *-er*.

   easy → easier   early → earlier   happy → happier

If the adjective ends in a consonant + vowel + consonant, we double the final consonant and add -er.

big → *bigger*   *sad* → *sadder*   *thin* → *thinner*

3 With longer adjectives (more than two syllables), we don't change the adjective – we put *more* in front of it.

expensive → *more* *expensive*
difficult → *more* *difficult*
interesting → *more* *interesting*

4 Some adjectives are irregular – they have a different comparative form.

good → *better*   *bad* → *worse*   *far* → *further*

Superlative adjectives

1 When we compare something with two or more other things, we use a superlative form with *the*.
Steve is the tallest boy in our class.
Brazil is the biggest country in South America.

2 With short adjectives, we normally add -est.

tall → *the tallest*   *short* → *the shortest*
old → *the oldest*   *clean* → *the cleanest*

Spelling rules for the -est ending are the same as for the -er ending in the comparative form.

nice → *nicest*   *happy* → *the happiest*
safe → *the safest*   *big* → *the biggest*
easy → *the easiest*   *thin* → *the thinnest*

3 With longer adjectives (more than two syllables), we don't change the adjective – we put *the most* in front of it.

delicious → *the most* *delicious*
important → *the most* *important*
intelligent → *the most* *intelligent*
This is the most important day of my life.
It's the most expensive shop in town.

4 Some adjectives are irregular.

good → *the best*   *bad* → *the worst*   *far* → *the furthest*
Saturday is the best day of the week.
My team is the worst team in the world!

can / can't (ability)

1 We use *can / can't* + the base form of the verb to talk about someone's ability to do something. The form of *can / can't* is the same for every person.

My father can lift 100 kg.   *I can't lift heavy things.*
I can swim 5 kilometres.   *My brother can't swim.*
He can write in Chinese.   *She can't spell.*

2 To make questions, we use *Can* + subject + base form of the verb. Short answers are formed with *Yes / No* + pronoun + *can* or *can't*.

Can your sister swim?   *Yes, she can.*
Can you lift 50 kilos?   *No, I can't.*

UNIT 10
be going to for plans and intentions

1 We use *be going to* to talk about things we intend to do in the future.

I'm going to visit my grandfather tomorrow.
My sister's going to study German at university.

2 The form is the present simple of *be* + *going to* + base form of the verb.

I'm going to stay at home on Sunday. I'm not going to go out.
She's going to look around the shops. She isn't going to buy anything.
Are you going to watch the film?
Is he going to give us homework tonight?

Short answers are formed using *Yes / No* + pronoun + the correct form of *be* (positive or negative).

Present continuous for future arrangements

We can use the present continuous to talk about arrangements for the future.

We're having a party next weekend. (It's organised.)
I'm meeting my friends in the park tomorrow. (I talked to my friends and we agreed to meet.)
Our parents are going on holiday in Spain next month. (They have their airline tickets and hotel reservation.)

Adverbs

1 Adverbs usually go with verbs – they describe an action:

We walked home slowly.   *The train arrived late.*
Drive carefully!

2 A lot of adverbs are formed by adjective + -ly.

quiet → *quietly*   *bad* → *badly*   *polite* → *politely*

If the adjective ends in -le, we drop the -e and add -y.

terrible → *terribly*   *comfortable* → *comfortably*

If the adjective ends in consonant + -y, we change the -y to -i and add -ly.

easy → *easily*   *happy* → *happily*   *lucky* → *luckily*

3 Some adverbs are irregular – they don't have an -ly ending.

good → *well*   *fast* → *fast*   *hard* → *hard*
early → *early*   *late* → *late*
I played well last week.   *He worked hard all day.*
She ran very fast.

4 Adverbs usually come immediately after the verb, or, if the verb has an object, after the object.

She sings well.   *She plays the piano well.*

UNIT 11
will / won't for future predictions

1 We use *will* (*'ll*) and *won't* to make predictions about the future.

When I'm older, I'll travel round the world. I won't stay here!
I'm sure you'll pass the test tomorrow. The questions won't be very difficult.
In the future, people will take holidays on Mars. But people won't live there.

2 We use *will / won't* + base form of the verb, and the form is the same for all subjects. We don't use any form of *do* in the negative.

You'll pass the test.   You won't pass the test.
He'll pass the test.   He won't pass the test.

3 Questions are formed with *will* + subject + base form of the verb. Again, we don't use any form of *do* in questions or short answers.

Will Andrea go to university?
Yes, she will. / No, she won't.
Will your friends come to the party?
Yes, they will. / No, they won't.

First conditional

1 In conditional sentences there are two clauses, an *if* clause and a result clause. We use the first conditional when it is possible or likely that the situation in the *if* clause will happen in the future.

If I pass the test, my parents will be happy. (= It's possible that I will pass, but I'm not sure.)
If it doesn't rain, we'll go for a walk. (= Perhaps it will rain, but I'm not sure.)

2 The *if* clause is formed with *If* + subject + present simple. The result clause is formed with subject + *will* + base form of the verb. There is a comma after the *if* clause.

If we have time, we'll do some shopping.
If you don't start your homework soon, you won't finish it tonight.

3 We can change the order of the two clauses. In this case, there is no comma between the clauses.

We'll do some shopping if we have time.
You won't finish your homework if you don't start it tonight.

Time clauses with *when / as soon as*

In sentences about the future, we use the present tense after *when* or *as soon as*, and the *will* future in the main clause. (The structure of these sentences is very like the structure of 1st conditional sentences.)

When I'm 18, I'll go to university.
I'll call you as soon as I get there.

UNIT 12
Present perfect simple with *ever / never*

1 We often use the present perfect to talk about things from the beginning of our life until now.

Sandro has travelled to a lot of different countries. (= from when he was born until now)
I haven't met your parents. (= at any time in my life, from when I was born until now)

2 When we use the present perfect with this meaning, we often use *ever* (= *at any time in someone's life*) in questions, and *never* (= *not ever*) in sentences. *Ever* comes between the noun or pronoun and the past participle. *Never* comes immediately after *have / has*.

Have you ever eaten Thai food?
I've never been interested in cooking.
Has he ever won a prize in a competition?
She's never tried to learn another language.

3 The present perfect is formed with the present tense of *have* + past participle of the main verb. For regular verbs, the past participle has the same *-ed* ending as the past simple. Irregular verbs have different past participles.

Regular verbs	Irregular verbs
*We've **stayed** in Athens three times.*	*We've **been** there three times.*
*Have they ever **climbed** a mountain?*	*Have they ever **flown** in a plane?*

See page 128 for the past participles of irregular verbs.

4 There is a difference between *been* and *gone*.

*I've **been** to the supermarket = I went to the supermarket and now <u>I am back again</u>.*
*They've **gone** to the supermarket = they went to the supermarket and <u>they are still there</u>.*

Present perfect vs. past simple

Both the **present perfect** and the **past simple** refer to the past. But we use the **past simple** to talk about situations or actions at a particular time in the past, and we use the **present perfect** to talk about situations or actions in the past, at an unspecified time between the past and now.

Past simple
I ate sushi two weeks ago.
I read a Shakespeare play last month.
He was late for school yesterday.
We didn't buy anything in town on Saturday.

Present perfect
I've eaten sushi a lot of times.
I've read six Shakespeare plays.
He's been late to school four times.
We haven't bought anything in town for a long time.

IRREGULAR VERBS

Base form	Past simple	Past participle
be	was / were	been
become	became	become
begin	began	begun
break	broke	broken
bring	brought	brought
build	built	built
buy	bought	bought
can	could	-
catch	caught	caught
choose	chose	chosen
come	came	come
cost	cost	cost
cut	cut	cut
do	did	done
draw	drew	drawn
drink	drank	drunk
drive	drove	driven
eat	ate	eaten
fall	fell	fallen
feel	felt	felt
find	found	found
fly	flew	flown
forget	forgot	forgotten
get	got	got
give	gave	given
go	went	gone
grow	grew	grown
have	had	had
hear	heard	heard
hit	hit	hit
keep	kept	kept
know	knew	known
leave	left	left

Base form	Past simple	Past participle
lend	lent	lent
lie	lay	lain
lose	lost	lost
make	made	made
mean	meant	meant
meet	met	met
pay	paid	paid
put	put	put
read /riːd/	read /red/	read /red/
ride	rode	ridden
run	ran	run
say	said	said
see	saw	seen
sell	sold	sold
send	sent	sent
show	showed	shown
sing	sang	sung
sit	sat	sat
sleep	slept	slept
speak	spoke	spoken
spend	spent	spent
stand	stood	stood
swim	swam	swum
take	took	taken
teach	taught	taught
tell	told	told
think	thought	thought
throw	threw	thrown
understand	understood	understood
wake	woke	woken
wear	wore	worn
win	won	won
write	wrote	written